NOBODY'S SOLDIER

THE LIFE OF ANDRII ANTONENKO

An Autobiography

AS TOLD TO

PETER ANTONENKO

Published in Australia by Sid Harta Publishers Pty Ltd,
ABN: 46 119 415 842
23 Stirling Crescent, Glen Waverley, Victoria 3150 Australia
Telephone: +61 3 9560 9920, Facsimile: +61 3 9545 1742
E-mail: author@sidharta.com.au

First published in Australia 2019
This edition published 2019
Copyright © Peter Antonenko 2019
Cover design, typesetting: WorkingType (www.workingtype.com.au)

The right of Andrii Antonenko to be identified as the Author of the Work has been asserted in accordance with the Copyright, Designs and Patents Act 1988.

The Author of this book accepts all responsibility for the contents and absolves any other person or persons involved in its production from any responsibility or liability where the contents are concerned.

Antonenko, Andrii
Nobody's Soldier: An Autobiography
ISBN: 978-1-925230-60-4
pp280

You can
loca'

This book is the story of one person's life – a person born in the
peaceful country area of the Ukraine in 1922 - a story that should
be read by everyone. The first chapter treats the reader to the
peaceful and idyllic life style of the Ukrainian people when their
country was at peace. As the story unfolds we learn first-hand
of the horrors of Joseph Stalin's communist rule of the Ukraine
commencing in 1929.

It is hard to believe than any one person could have endured
so much trauma and survived, but survive he did, long enough
for one of his sons to tell his amazing story.

— **Valerie J. Griffiths**

Conflicts between Ukraine and Russia have been well recorded
throughout history. But living here in Australia, it is hard to imagine a life lived by people who were caught up in wars that were
based on greed and political motivation.

No-one at the age of seven years old should have to wait
three days for their father to turn up after an interrogation
by political police, pistol whipped and beaten. It was at that
moment that Andrii's life changed forever and it became a hell
on earth to flee Russian occupation under the communist lead-
ership of Joseph Stalin.

Andrii's story is heartbreaking and shows the immense cruelty
humans can inflict upon one another. His story is a wonderful
tribute to human endurance, hope and tenacity.

Andrii's story fills me wit
ship people will endure to fir
— **John Morrow's Pick of**

This book is a must for anyone interested in the human impact of Stalinism and the Second World War in Ukraine and its aftermath with the start of the end of the British Empire and the attitudes of the British population of the day towards others. The story of Andrii Antonenko carries on the great tradition of resilience resourcefulness and perseverance of migrants that have enriched our nation so much.

 —**Keith Gregory author of "Gaunasala Ni Bula "**

A fascinating page-turning account of resilience and the will to live, Nobody's Soldiers tells the story of Ukraine-born Andrii Antonenko's earlier years. In the face of the cruelty of Stalinist oppression and the horrors of war, Andrii displays the nobility of the human spirit in his struggle to survive against almost overwhelming forces. This is a well told and inspiring tale which has the reader glued to the text, needing to know what happens next. A great example of an ordinary person never giving up and doing extraordinary things.

 — **Noel Braun author**

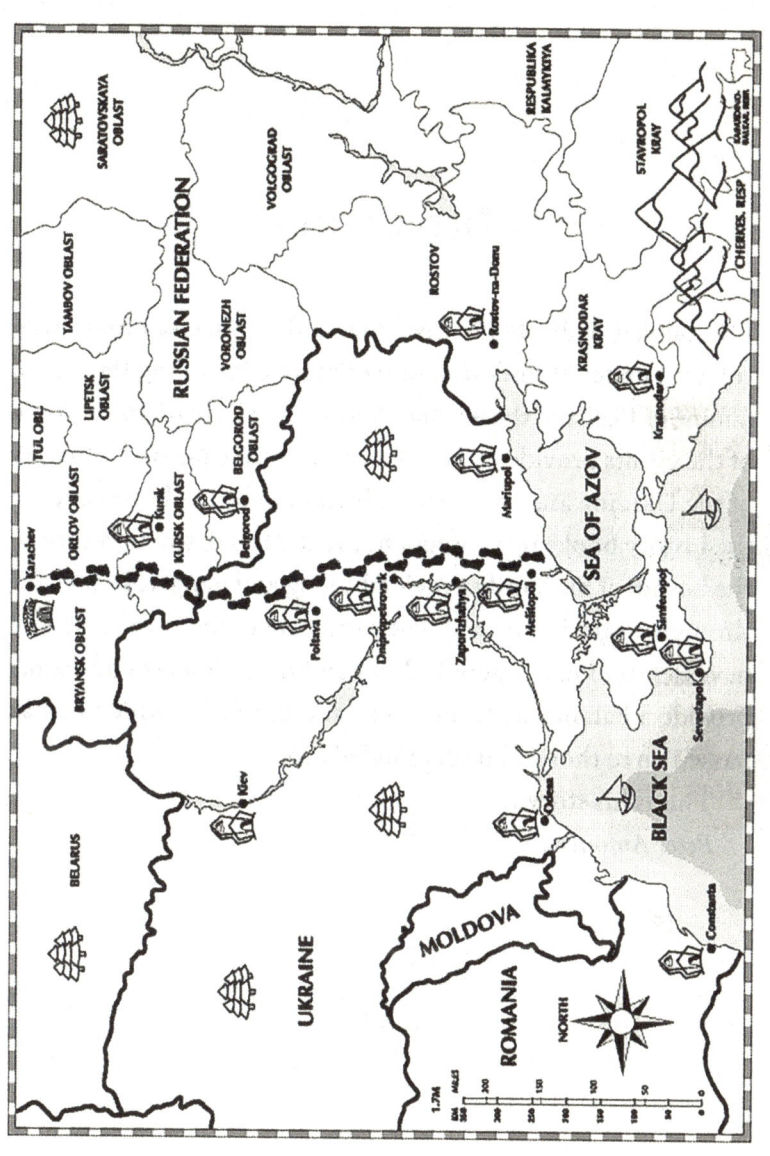

Modern day Ukraine and surrounds

v

DEDICATION

This book is dedicated to my father and all the Ukrainians who suffered under Stalin's totalitarian regime including the forced famine of 1933 and the Second World War. His firsthand account of the events provide a snapshot of a critical time in the history of the Ukraine and the events which have been glossed over in the history books by subsequent events. His desire to return to the bosom of his family provided a long and dangerous journey through a number of countries and experiences which would have defeated many people. His candid and honest comments provide a balance of compassion and optimism which he has passed on to those who surrounded him.

This is his story…

Peter Antonenko

Acknowledgments

Thanks are due to Prue Drever and Faye Baxter with their input with the initial version of this book. Guy Murfey provided inspiration and guidance to ensure this project got off the ground. Ronald Francis is to be thanked for his insistence that this was an important story to be shared. My wife Julia provided love and encouragement throughout.

PREFACE

I was about seven and a half years old when my father came home after three days of interrogation in jail. He had been pistol-whipped and beaten by the political police and his head bore the scars of his savage beating. I will always remember the sight of dried blood on my father's head and body and my mother bitterly weeping. It was the end of the world I had known and the beginning of a life spent fleeing the horrors of Soviet occupation, starvation and certain death.

My father, an honest and hard-working man, dared to oppose the communist regime directive that he give up the land which had belonged to his family for generations and join a collective farm. Such violent punishment was not uncommon in those days and was a sign of things to come as countries behind the "iron curtain" felt the chilling touch of Joseph Stalin and his far-reaching communist tentacles.

The history of Ukraine is peppered with periods of occupation—by many different forces—for many centuries. In 1709, the Russian army of Czar Peter invaded Ukraine. The much smaller Ukrainian army, led by the famous Hetman and Cossack nobleman, Ivan Mazeppa, was joined by King Charles XII of Sweden's army and the two forces battled the Russians near a place called Poltava, in central Ukraine. King Charles was badly wounded and, losing heart, the Swedes retreated, leaving the Ukrainians to fight alone. It was a massacre and Russia had little trouble taking the rest of Ukraine.

For many years Ukrainians fought to become an independent nation despite long periods battling communist Russians, Czarist Russians, Poles, Rumanians and Germans, as well as other armies further back in time. In 1920 Ukraine declared independence, but was again forcibly taken by Russia. On 24 August 1991, Ukraine again declared independence and after the disintegration of the Soviet Union, became the largest complete nation in Europe.

Russian communist leader Joseph Stalin's rise to power in 1924 and the adoption of communism by Russia was the start of very hard times. In 1929-1930, the Soviet regime began the process of collectivisation in Ukraine and farmers and their families were forced to give up their livelihoods to the collective farms. They worked for very little money and food. There was no food at all for those too sick or old to work. These poor people were called "enemies of the state" and the workers were forbidden to care for or feed them. Those who tried to resist were called *kulaks*, a Russian word meaning "independent", but in a derogatory way as it also means "enemy". The Soviets would not tolerate *kulaks* and set about destroying these families.

As if a history filled with bloodshed and oppression was not enough, in 1932-1933 a famine raged in Ukraine and millions of people died of starvation. This tragedy was man-made and was deliberately caused by the communist government as a punishment for the Ukrainian farming communities, most of whom tried to resist collectivisation.

Before this terrible crime, Ukraine had suffered through famine because of wars, but never on the same scale. The earth still gave crops, but the NKVD, who were in charge of this operation organised gangs of communist youths to take every scrap of food from the country people. Nobody dared say a word. They raided houses, barns, stables and any other place they thought food might be hidden—they even probed the ground with thin steel rods looking for hidden food. The Party, the farmers were told, needed the food and that was that. Everyone knew what happened to people who spoke out against the Party.

There would never have been a truly natural famine. Ukraine, with its rich black fertile soil and many natural treasures has for many centuries been known as the "bread basket of Europe".

The Russian leaders hated us Ukrainians and were envious of our beautiful country. Millions of Ukrainians died in the famine and those who didn't were forced to work for the Soviets before and during the Second World War, and for the Germans after they occupied the country. Most of Ukraine's writers, composers, scientists, and church leaders were destroyed by the communists, either by being sent to places like Siberia or by execution because they, too, tried to resist the communist domination of Ukraine.

Since the introduction of communism, much of the Ukrainian soil, air and water has been badly contaminated. I know it is a very different place from the homeland I remember from my childhood. I have spoken to many Ukrainians living in Australia who returned to their former home and, without exception, they were all bitterly disappointed by what the Russians left behind.

Chernobyl, the scene of a disastrous nuclear accident in 1986, is only about 100 kilometers north of our capital city, Kiev. This disaster is well-known across the world, thanks to media attention—less well known is how much more of the country has been ruined by pollution and the type of neglect that many people believe caused the disaster at the nuclear plant. In the same way that this devastating occurrence ruined much more than the people and elements in its immediate area, so too has communism destroyed the very essence of Ukraine and its people.

Many of my family perished as a direct result of communism. I survived despite being forced into labour camps and children's homes throughout my adolescence, being shot during the war and contracting tuberculosis.

This is my story...

Andrii Antonenko March 2001

BOOK I

Growing Up

CHAPTER I

Life on the farm

I was born in a peaceful Ukrainian fishing village called Stepanivka on the coast of the Azov Sea, in 1922. I don't know the exact date, but believe it was at the beginning of September. I remember Stepanivka was a beautiful village, about 800 kilometres from the capital city, Kiev. In those days there were about 2000 villagers, most of whom were farmers. All the farming families were self-sufficient, growing crops to feed themselves and their animals throughout the year, trading other goods at the market and only having to buy things such as needles from the village store.

I lived there with my family: father Jacob; mother Kateriana; paternal grandfather Abraham; and eight brothers and sisters. Sidor was my eldest brother; then Tatyana, my eldest sister; Paula; Timothy and Alexandra. My brother, Alexi, who was about ten years old when I was born, came next, followed by Frossia, my youngest sister, myself and Michael, who was two years younger than me.

Our twenty-seven acre farm was about three kilometres away from the village, and our house was on about one acre, which went from the main street of the village right down to the sea. We had a variety of animals including two cows and a calf, two horses and two foals, ten sheep, three pigs, lots of chickens, ducks and pigeons. We grew wheat, barley, oats, sunflowers, melons, lucerne (alfalfa) and flax for making linen. Sometimes we grew other crops, but these were the main ones. Like a lot of other families, we also had a small fishing boat with oars and sometimes my father, whom we called Tato, would take us younger children out on the seas to put down nets or to check on the nets already out there.

The village had two unsealed streets; one wide one, alongside which was our house, and one much smaller one. The roads were only ever used by horse-drawn carts and sleighs in winter. In the middle of our street were five wells. Although most farms had their own water, we used that for the animals and drank from the street wells ourselves. Women usually collected the water from the wells, using a yoke across their shoulders to make it easier to carry two buckets. Drawing water from these wells was a social occasion, a time for the women to catch up on gossip and exchange jokes, stories and any village news. The village also had three shops, a school, five windmills for making flour, a small factory for processing sunflower oil, a council building and a church with a cemetery at the back.

Most of the houses were made of mud bricks, with ordinary house bricks around the bottom of the outside walls and around the window frames. Nearly everyone whitewashed the mud bricks with lime every spring, just before Easter. Some people even painted permanent flowers and other designs on the bricks around the window frames. Most houses, including ours, had a clay-type floor, which had to be resurfaced three times a year. Wood was scarce and only those who could afford to bring the wood from Melitopol, forty kilometres away, had wooden floors.

Our house was quite typical of that era. We had a bathhouse, a stable for the animals in winter, a store shed, hay shed, and a bungalow where my grandfather lived. There were lots of fruit trees and a large area, which we called the field, to grow our crops. The entire yard near the house and farm buildings was covered with finely crushed sea shells. They were so fine that they didn't cut the animals' feet, but if we children fell on them we ended up with scraped elbows and knees.

The house was built on one acre, and had two huge rooms; a bed-sitting room and a kitchen. Mama and Tato slept in the bedroom at night and it was used as a sitting room during the day. We children slept in the kitchen, sometimes on top of the stove or on shelf-like beds, which could be stored away during the day. Through a door in the kitchen we could step straight into the stable, where we kept the animals during bad weather. From the stable we could walk straight into the wheat store and an outdoor toilet. Sometimes, if we had a newborn calf or foal, Mama would put straw in the kitchen near the stove so the babies had a few days of warmth and comfort, especially if the weather was very cold. When she went outside, most of the animals would follow Mama around as she often gave them an extra slice of bread or lump of sugar; especially the horses, which she loved.

Near the house we had a bath house with two rooms. The first one was the warm room where we undressed. A stove served both rooms, which were divided by a fireproof brick wall. The part of the stove in the second room had a long metal plate which would become very hot and water was sprinkled on it to make steam. There were two shelves, the highest one being the hottest. Very thin branches were tied together so bathers could gently beat themselves to help circulation. Water in a wooden bucket could then be poured over a person. Cool or warm water, whichever you wished to use. In winter some people would go naked from the steam room straight out into the snow and roll in it. My brother, Alexi, kept pigeons and they would sit on the inside of the roof in the bath house. One day a skunk got in among the pigeons and the smell killed more than half the birds.

In that area of the property we had two large mulberry trees. One had dark red berries and the other had white berries and when the fruit was ready, we children would climb the trees and shake the fruit down. Our father put a large piece of wood from one mulberry tree to the other and hung a swing from it, so we and our friends could play on it. As well as all our farm animals, we also had a very big old dog called Pirate. He had a big kennel near the house and was very gentle. When I had some pastries, I would eat the cherries, mulberries or cheese and give the pastry to Pirate. Sometimes I would sit at the back of his kennel and he would sit in front and nobody would know my hiding place. One day I took all Tato's nails and hammered them into the ground so he couldn't find them. When I eventually told him where they were he pulled my ear, because it was very difficult for him to get the nails out.

All Ukrainian farmers and their families worked hard on the farms until the older children married or moved away. The small children would feed the fowls and other animals, especially the babies. They would also bring in straw to help keep the stove going, but once we started school, it was school and homework first. There were a few families who were lazy, which resulted in them having very little of anything. Although they were disapproved of, my family and other villagers would give them food and drink on special occasions, such as Christmas and Easter, mostly for their children's sake. I remember one man who was an alcoholic. One day he drove down our street in a two-wheeled horse-drawn cart but he couldn't control the horse and it seemed the horse had had enough of him. It finally stood on its hind legs, tipping him out on to the road. He wasn't hurt, but we kids thought it was hilarious.

* * *

My parents were very hardworking, honest, honourable and religious. I remember them as being old-fashioned, even for those days. My father was strict, but not overly so, and the younger children got away with much more than the older ones. Sometimes we were smacked, but not very often and only if we deserved it. Sometimes Tato gave us a light tug on the ear or hair to show his disapproval of us. When Mama slapped us she would cry, thinking she had hit us too hard, but her smacks were so light it was like being brushed by a fly. We did have to behave at the table though, because food was honoured and had to be worked hard for, although we never went short of food.

The older I get the more it amazes me how hard my parents worked every day. They had no more than four hours sleep every night because there was so much to do. My eldest brother, Sidor, had married and moved away, as had several others in my family, so there was more work left for Tato, Mama and my brother Alexi to do. Frossia, my youngest sister, did some light jobs and Mama also taught her household and farm duties. Besides the usual house and farm work, attending to Grandfather and looking after the young children, there were also animals to be cared for. Mama did the milking, and Tato made many things for us and the property. He also made and repaired fishing nets and started teaching us boys this as well.

Mama made bread, butter, cheese, sauces, jams, pickled vegetables and lots of other things and sometimes during the summer when she had time she would make ice-cream and put it down the well to cool. In the winter, when it was too cold to be outdoors, Mama would prepare wool for knitting jumpers, hats, scarves, gloves, socks and baby clothing on her spinning wheel. Once the flax had been washed, thrashed and combed by the rest of the family, Mama would weave the linen thread on her home weaver and use a Singer peddle sewing machine to make shirts, trousers, towels, tablecloths, handkerchiefs, tea cloths and cloths to drape around our religious icons. The girls would help her and make lacework and embroider many items.

My brother Michael and I were too young to do much work

around the farm, so we had a pretty normal childhood; lots of scrapes and a few accidents. In summer time, we would play on the seashore with our friends, and about three times a week Frossia and I would go to the seaside and collect small shrimp-like crustaceans to feed our ducks.

Sometimes we would go out in our father's boat. One day in the early morning we were out checking the nets and I became very seasick because of the choppy weather. Tato jokingly said, 'Don't become seasick or I'll throw you overboard.' I also remember one day when a boy threw a stone, hitting me on the head and causing quite a lot of blood to flow. Grandfather saw this from inside his bungalow and came outside shouting and waving his walking stick, but the boy ran away and Grandfather was too old to chase him very far.

One accident I had at an early age could well have been my last. We had almost finished bringing in the harvest and I was riding on the cultivator plough drawn by two horses. One of my older brothers was leading the horses and I was standing up on the metal part when I slipped and fell under the blade. The blade cut my back, but my brother stopped the horses as soon as he realised something was wrong. I was about five years old at the time and do not remember everything that happened. I was picked up and cloths were wrapped around my wound to stop the bleeding. The doctor lived seven kilometres away in the next village and I was taken there as quickly as possible in a light horse-drawn cart. The doctor stitched me up and said I was lucky not to have been killed. Being a young healthy boy I healed very quickly because, even though the injury was quite deep, it was still only a flesh wound.

One day my mother wanted to cut my hair. I, like most six-year-old boys, didn't want to have my hair cut so I escaped and walked seven kilometres to my maternal grandparents' house in the next village. My grandparents had a very big pear tree, which seemed to me to nearly always be covered with thousands of small but very juicy pears. Someone saw me and told my parents. They sent Alexi to bring me home in a light pony cart and I received a spanking as well as a haircut.

* * *

I remember Ukraine being a very seasonal place, and I loved all the seasons. Spring was always my favourite, when the snow had melted and millions of beautiful wild flowers of many types and colours would appear. Storks would arrive to nest on some of the villagers' roofs. These birds were thought to bring good luck and healthy children, so no one ever harmed them. The owner of a roof where storks chose to make their home was considered very lucky indeed and the delighted house occupants would erect a small cartwheel on the roof for the storks to make their nest on. There was a very old legend that if storks were not allowed to nest where they chose, or were harmed in any way, they would bring hot ashes and burn the house down. We never knew if there was any truth in this, but the villagers didn't want to tempt fate because many houses had thatched roofs. We younger children would also build bird boxes for the smaller birds and put them in the trees.

The fruit trees would be covered in blossom and everywhere there would be a mass of colour. Millions of brightly-coloured butterflies would also appear and a great variety of birds flew in from Africa, Turkey, Greece and other southern countries. Along both sides of the street there were many acacia trees, and in spring they had huge hanging bunches of snow-white blossoms, which smelt like honey and tasted very sweet. We children would often gorge ourselves on them, but we had to be careful of the small thorns. The average temperature would be fifteen to sixteen degrees Celsius from March to May.

By May, the weather would be a little warmer — about twenty-three degrees Celsius — and the first cherries would appear. As summer took hold, the fruit harvesting would begin and I would roam around, smelling the fresh clean air, often sleeping outside under the apple or mulberry trees and eating lots of cherries. The sea was very shallow for about 200 metres and when we went out in the boat, we could look over the side and see right down to the seabed. There were days in summer and early autumn when it became very hot — sometimes as high as thirty-five to thirty-eight degrees Celsius — and we would often have very fierce thunderstorms which could be seen from kilometres away. The domestic animals would become very frightened. When the storm struck, the sea would look very different, rough and dirty as the storm raged.

The late autumn months were a lot cooler, but I enjoyed it all. The leaves on the trees would turn red, orange and gold and, when they dropped, we children would wrap up warmly and play in the leaves, kicking and throwing them in the air. The grown-ups would prepare the fruit, vegetables, fish and meat for winter. As winter approached the trees would become covered in snow; they looked sparkling and beautiful. We would kick and shake the trees, bringing the snow down upon us. Sometimes, if there was fog and frost, ice would form on the branches and long icicles would hang down from the roof of our house.

Often in winter, as soon as there was enough snow, we would ride in one or two-horse open sleighs to go visiting or to church. We would put hay or straw in the bottom and wrap up well with sheep skin coats, fur hats and gloves and cover ourselves with home-made blankets. It was very cold — between ten and twenty degrees below zero — and sometimes the sea would freeze and we would go skating on the frozen surface. I'm not sure if the Azov Sea was frozen all the way to Kuban, but I believe it often was, because I remember seeing horse-drawn sleighs travelling on the sea ice. We children would also make a snow 'grandmother', something like a snowman. At times when the snow was very dry, we would wear long boots made of very thick stiff felt, which could not be bent in any way. These boots were no good in slushy snow as they were not waterproof.

We spent a lot of time indoors, but once we started school we walked 500 metres to and from the schoolhouse, no matter how cold it was. One thing I remember about winter is how much I enjoyed looking at the window panes, on which the frost had made patterns which looked like stars, fern leaves and trees.

* * *

Our family belonged — and still does — to the Ukrainian Orthodox religion, which is the state religion of Ukraine. When I was a young boy, and to this day, the greater majority of the population of Ukraine were and are Ukrainian Orthodox. In the 1920s there were also quite a few Greek, Bulgarian, Serbian, Russian and other orthodox groups. Most of the Ukrainians who practiced the Ukrainian Greek Catholic religion lived in Western Ukraine, near the borders of Poland, Hungary and Czechoslovakia. In the past, Poland had occupied this area of Ukraine and forced their religion on the native people. There have always been many Jewish people in Ukraine; there were three Jewish families living in my village. They had to go to Melitopol to worship at their synagogue, forty kilometres away.

The principles of the Ukrainian Orthodox religion are similar in many ways to most Christian religions, with Easter and Christmas being the special times of the year. For Orthodox Ukrainians, Christmas day falls on the 7th of January and New Year on the 14th of January. This is because our church still follows the old calendar for its church celebrations. In those days, the women folk would spend weeks preparing food and we would visit other houses in the village carol singing and chanting blessings for each person's home.

The night before Christmas, Saint Nicholas would put gifts of apples, nuts and home-made sweets under the children's pillows. On Christmas morning, most people went to church. The women of the family had been preparing for the midday meal for quite a while and would have strewn fresh hay on the floor and under the icons in honour of baby Jesus and his mother Mary. A barley pudding and pudding made from dried cooked fruits were also placed in separate large bowls under the icons on a small table. The whole house would smell fresh and clean from the aromatic fragrance of the hay. Incense, made from the sap of pine trees, would be burnt in small amounts on the fire.

After the meal the older people rested then would go visiting relatives and friends. In the evening the children went out carol singing for friends and relatives. One of us would carry a star-shaped lantern on a long pole with a candle in it. We would be invited in to sing and were given small gifts, usually home-made sweets, nuts and apples.

For the New Year we children, along with our friends, would go to relatives and friends' houses singing "Happy New Year" and blessings for them, their possessions and for the next year's crop. We would throw mixed grain over the icons and sprinkle it around the rooms while singing the blessings. The grown-ups then would give us sweets, apples, biscuits, nuts and small amounts of money. The apples would have been kept in the cool room for special occasions such as Christmas and New Year.

Easter is also a very special time for us. Ukrainian churches are always beautifully decorated with religious paintings and icons draped with embroidered cloths with crocheted edging and many other colourful trappings. We also have fresh flowers when available. For special occasions like Easter, extra deco-rations are added. The priest wears very handsome colourful vestments, and he changes to blue and yellow ones — the Ukrai-nian colours — once Christ has risen. His clothing and mitre are heavily embroidered with gold thread and encrusted with different coloured gem stones and small religious pictures. The people in my village would wear their very best clothes, blouses with lots of embroidery and colourful scarves and shawls, and some people would wear national dress.

On the evening of Easter Saturday, the service would begin at about nine pm and continue until about two am on Easter Sunday. The priest and his assistants stayed all night, but the congregation would come and go as they please. Our church was in the mid-dle of the village and only 300 metres from our house. Nobody slept much, even the children who were not too young stayed up. When I was young, the church would be lit by hundreds of candles and it would be surprisingly warm. At midnight the bells would ring to show Christ had risen and everybody would go outside. When electricity was introduced, everyone would gather outside the church waiting for the letters 'XB' to light up in bulbs. Bells would ring and people would kiss each other on both cheeks, saying *Xpucmos Bockpec* ("Christ has risen") and answering *Boict Nhy Bockpec* ("He has indeed").

People would bring baskets to be blessed by the priest, contain-ing beautifully coloured and patterned eggs, high Easter cakes with coloured seeds on top (most people put their candle on the cake) and garlic to keep away any evil spirits. People also add extra things such as salami, ham, fruit and even wine or whisky. These baskets are covered by embroidered cloths until the time of the blessing. Years ago the tradition was that the food and drink was made or grown yourself.

The priest, his assistants, the choir and anyone wanting to join in would walk clockwise around the church three times, the assistants carrying religious banners and icons, the people singing and carrying lighted candles. The priest would bless all the people and the baskets by sprinkling them and their baskets with holy water on a whisk made of willow strands from a silver chalice held by one of the assistants. Once the blessing of the people and food was finished everyone would go home, where a lovely embroidered Easter tablecloth would be spread on the table and everyone could eat the blessed food for breakfast.

When I was young there were twelve different foods for us to eat in the old Ukrainian tradition. I always felt happy at this time as my family and all the other villagers were also happy that Christ had risen.

* * *

When I was six years old, my second oldest sister, Paula, who was about twenty years old, married her childhood sweetheart, Sanko. Everyone in the village attended. The bridal party and many other people wore beautifully embroidered national Ukrainian costumes, the girls wearing flowers in their hair and long multi-coloured ribbons in their head dresses.

Special light carts drawn by two horses were used to take the bride and bridegroom to church. The carts were beautifully decorated and so were the horses, who wore coloured paper chains, flowers and brightly embroidered hankies tied to their halters. After the church service, the special carts with the bride and groom came first, followed by the best man and bride's attendants, with the musicians, family members and friends following, paraded around the village and then on to the bride's house. Mama then threw sweets, nuts and small change over everyone. The feast was held both inside and outside the house with plenty of food and drink, and singing and dancing in the streets. When this was over, the bride and groom collected her belongings, so that he could start to take her to his parents' house until their own house was ready. However, they are traditionally stopped by young men who hold the horses' heads and won't let them go through the gate until the bridegroom finds a bottle of alcohol to bribe them with.

It was usual in Ukrainian families for a bridegroom's parents to give the couple a block of land to build their new home on. The bride's parents would give them farming land and both sets of parents would give whatever farm animals they could spare. Both families would also help build on the new land to get the new couple off to a good start in life. Paula, Sanko and his parents lived at the other end of the village and after the wedding I would often go over to see them. They all liked me and always gave me some homemade sweets and other food.

A few months after Paula and Sanco's wedding, I asked Mama if I could start school. She took me to see the headmaster, who said, 'Andrii is only six years old. He's too young. We don't take children until they are seven.' So I had to wait.

CHAPTER II

Collectively communist

IT WAS the winter of 1929-1930, a bitterly cold year, with a lot of snow and the winds blowing in very heavy gusts. It was this winter that the life I had always known was brutally destroyed by communists working under Russian leader Joseph Stalin's orders.

Previously, in the late spring of 1929, in a field outside our village, a Tiger Moth aircraft landed. Nobody in our area had ever seen an aircraft and the whole village ran outside to have a look. It had brought an important-looking person who we later discovered was a high-placed official in the government. He was dressed in a long leather coat, with leather straps across his shoulders, a leather document case hanging from his left side and a wooden holster, carrying a large long-barrelled pistol, from his right. I got a good look at it and found out later it was a German-type gun, called a Mauser. It was a very popular weapon among the communists, especially the NKVD. We stared at him unashamedly because to us he seemed very unusual, and under our stares he strutted importantly about. Looking back, I believe that he was probably a propaganda organiser and he was also our first taste of the collectivisation process that was to change all our lives forever.

Collectivisation was a system devised by Stalin and his communist regime from Russia. Under this system, farmers were forced to hand over their land and all it contained to the communist leaders who controlled the area. The farms were then joined together to become larger "collective" farms and the people were forced to work on these farms for very little money and food. Most people didn't want to give up everything they and their ancestors had worked hard for all their lives but unless they renounced their own way of life and joined the communists, there was no choice and resisters were often savagely beaten or killed. My father tried to resist and was taken away for three days. When he came home we could see he had been beaten and hit on the head with a pistol. I will never forget my mother's bitter tears and the sight of my father, with dried blood encrusting his head and shoulders. Although I didn't understand at the time, this was the beginning of the end for us.

Many other families in our village were forced out of their homes and off their land. Everything they had was taken by gangs of young communist hoodlums who had been sent down from the towns and cities to carry out the communist government's orders. We lost our furniture, farm animals and the farm machinery. All the larger items were taken to the collective farms and anything else was sold for next to nothing to people who had turned up to watch them devastate our home. We didn't have very much, but what we did have our whole family and our ancestors had worked very hard for. We were even more dismayed to find that people from our own village bought some of our belongings. Others came in and stole our few things and some were close neighbours whom we had looked upon as our friends. Although I was very young, I knew what they were doing and who they were and I have never forgiven them for stealing from my family. Many were lazy, good-for-nothing people who had always been envious of our family and other hard-working folk. We had often helped these people and that is one of the reasons why I find it hard to forgive them.

I don't remember Grandfather dying, but he was not with us when this was happening, so he must have already passed away before our lives were turned upside down. It would have broken his heart to see what happened to his family.

* * *

So, as the frozen winds of winter swirled around us, Mama, Tato, Alexi, Frossia, Michael and I were marched under guard away from our devastated home to the village square. Mama had managed to bring a few homemade blankets and we had our winter clothes on. We were only allowed to bring the clothes we were wearing and a few things we could carry, as well as a small amount of food and water. At the village square we saw about twenty other families, also under guard. The rest of our family had married or moved away, with the exception of Alexanda, and so they escaped this rounding up of the communist resistors, the *kulaks*, the "rich farmers who are enemies of the people". But we were not rich, nor were we anyone's "enemy", until the communists made us hate them, and we were certainly not the enemy of ordinary people.

The farming community were ordinary, hard-working people who loved their land and their way of life and quite naturally did not want to give up everything they had to the collective farms. Others, like my second eldest brother, Timothy, escaped the round-up because he was not a farmer. He had married the girl across the road, Tina, and because they were not farmers they lived in a different area. Tina's brother, Petro, was a very good friend of mine. But Tina's parents, who were farmers, lost everything, even the old windmill. Her father was taken to Siberia and never heard of again. Petro and his mother lived in a very poor, small house and I wasn't told why they hadn't been taken away at the same time as their father.

Our guards, who were soldiers of the NKVD and young civilian activist communists, gestured for us to climb into waiting horse-drawn sledges. Many people were crying noisily, especially the children. I can't remember if I cried, but I remember feeling very cold. Our escorts were mounted on horses and armed with rifles and handguns. We were told to get ready to move out; if anyone tried to escape they would be shot. They told us nothing about what would happen to us or where we were going and we were terribly frightened; I could feel the fear all around me. We were taken forty kilometres to the railway station at Melitopol, where a train made up of about fifty cattle trucks, or wagons, stood waiting. Each truck was to become "home" for five or six families. In the middle of our truck was a small black portable wood and coke-burning stove for some warmth. There was also a large bucket to be used as a toilet.

We spent about two weeks trapped inside the cattle truck with no idea of our destination. There were so many people crammed in that we could not move around much other than to use the toilet bucket. It was so cold that some people in other wagons died on the way. The guards, who were not with us but in proper carriages at the front and rear of the train, gave us very little food and the fumes from the burning coke were quite bad. The train stopped every day, always away from stations. With the guards standing nearby, two men from each truck would carry the toilet buckets and any dead bodies off the train and take aboard buckets of logs, coke and half-frozen water. Or, if there was no water, the buckets would be filled with snow. We were given small amounts of stale dark bread and salty fish to eat and we were sure that the salted fish was meant to make us thirstier and add to our torture. We never saw what the guards ate and drank but we could be sure it wasn't the same rubbish dished out to us.

We travelled more than 1600 kilometres through Ukraine and Russia to Moscow. After a further 1200 kilometres of lonely snow-covered forest, we reached our destination, Archangel, near the White Sea, which is very close to the Arctic Circle. In freezing conditions we were all unloaded and marched for about ten kilometres through a snow-covered forest to a large camp, where there were many large wooden barrack-type buildings. At least twenty families were housed in one of these barracks — about 200 people. Our beds were wooden shelves in three tiers — we had to climb ladders to get to the upper ones — and we were given no mattresses or bedclothes of any kind. It was so cold we had to sleep in our outdoor clothing. There was not much room for anything else in our barracks except two stoves, which were quite inadequate. There were many biting insects and when it was dark the insects would jump down from the roof and cause everyone much discomfort. When we squashed them, they made a dreadful smell.

Melted snow was used as drinking water but, when other water was needed, there was a hole in the snow-covered earth. When water was drawn up in a bucket on a rope, some of it would spill and freeze and because there were no protective walls it was very slippery and dangerous. Someone could easily have slipped down the hole and that would have been the end of them, but I never heard of this happening.

* * *

By the time we had been at the camp for six months, some people had escaped. Others were caught trying to escape and many were lost in the forest or marshes. The local people were told that if they caught anyone from the labour camp they were to give them up to the Secret Police. They would be given rewards of food and vodka for doing so. Conditions at the camp were terrible. We were getting very little food but at the end of spring 1930, as the snow was melting, my mother and sister were able to pick some red berries which were as big as peas and quite sour. There were lots of them; they looked like redcurrants and grew close to the ground in marshy forest areas. My youngest brother, Michael, had been quite ill and these berries were a big help to him. Tato and many of the other men were forced to cut down trees, while others would turn them into planks so that more barracks could be built. A two-handled two-man saw was used and as this was very hard work, these workers were allowed a little more food.

One day I was with my sister, Frossia, just outside the camp when we saw some people from another barracks carrying a box. It was a funeral procession. Now that the ground was softer, people were starting to bury their dead. People in the camp were dying all the time and during winter, there was no way to bury the bodies because the ground was too hard to dig. But despite the softer ground, the people carrying the box couldn't dig very deeply and when they left I saw what I thought was a big dog, standing some distance away. I pointed it out to Frossia, who told me it was a wolf and explained that it was waiting to dig up the body and eat it. That was the first time I had seen a wolf and when my sister explained how dangerous they were, I was rather worried that they were coming so close to where people were living.

* * *

During the summer of 1930, Mama and Tato decided that Alexi, Frossia and I should try to escape. They had saved as much food as possible for us to take with us. Michael was still sick so they would stay behind to care for him. Alexi was eighteen and our leader, Frossia was fourteen and I was eight. They gave Alexi the food and some water, instructions and advice and as many directions as they had been able to find out. They did everything they could to give us as good a chance as possible of escaping back to Ukraine. There were some guards at the camp but they were not as watchful as they could have been. They knew it was difficult for prisoners to escape because of the bad weather, wolves, marshes and hundreds of kilometres of snow-covered forests. It was also easy to get lost and many of the local folks were on the lookout for escapees in return for their rewards from the Secret Police. Also, most people in the camp were from Southern Ukraine, an area where there were no forests and the only groups of trees were orchards, so they were understandably too frightened to go into the forest. But we thought we had a better chance because the guards would not expect children to escape alone.

We were unbelievably lucky; we just walked into the forest one evening and travelled seven or eight kilometres to a railway line, which we knew was close by because we had heard the trains. We soon realised that not all the locals gave up escapees. Soon after we arrived at the railway line someone told Alexi which train to take to travel south, even though they must have realised we had escaped from the labour camp. We hid in one of the wagons on the train in between some logs, and even though it had become quite dark, we soon realised that we really were on the right train travelling south to Ukraine. We left this train just before Moscow and Alexi found out which goods train was going to Ukraine. We hid underneath some empty bags and travelled as far as Melitopil, about forty kilometres from our village of Stepanivka. There was no more railway line and we had to walk the rest of the way on an unmade country road.

It was very dangerous for Alexi and Frossia, but they took me to Stepanivka and left me with our elder sister Tatyana, and her husband Gregory. I heard later that Alexi had changed his name and gone down to the Caspian Sea, where he was working as a mechanic on board a ship. Frossia managed to get a job as a nanny in Crimea.

* * *

Tatyana and Gregory had four children, three girls and a boy. The boy's name was Fedor and he and I became very good friends. He always called me Uncle Andrii, even though he was only four years younger than me. We played and went to many places together. Tatyana was pleased to look after me, even though they were very poor, and I would have been happy there if it had not been for her husband, Gregory, who was the village council clerk and who used to beat me with his belt quite often for no special reason. I was happy that he didn't beat Tatyana or his own children.

After I arrived at my sister's place I started school. Every day, outside the school, we had to wipe our shoes and be inspected for clean hands. I liked school and did well, but I remember that on one occasion, when I'd been throwing paper balls and pinching one of the girls, I had to kneel on broken dried peas in the corner of the room as punishment. The other children thought it was very funny. Some of the older boys used to smoke behind the toilets. The teachers could smell it and gave them a lecture on how bad smoking was for their health.

I was quite happy at school but because of the beatings I received from my sister's husband I decided to leave after about three months. I went to the seaside where there was a small fish processing shed, but someone told Gregory they had seen me, so he came after me. He took me back home and beat me; he just didn't like me, I don't know why. He would hit me on the head and ears quite hard and I instinctively realised that this could be quite dangerous. Two weeks later I left home again and walked to my maternal grandparents' farm in the next village, but when I arrived I discovered they had also been taken away. Instead, there was a small collective farm and two women who were milking cows gave me a job looking after the calves. I didn't mind the job but only stayed a couple of days because all they had at meal times was milk, cottage cheese and bread. They never had any other sort of food and I soon got fed up with it. One of their jobs I remember was hoisting a black sack on the top of a long pole to let the workers know when it was meal time.

I had nowhere to go now that my grandparents had disappeared. Although my sister, Paula, and her husband, Sanko, both liked me and had been happy to see me when I visited them in the past, Sanko was an army man and had become an officer. The Soviet authorities had forced him to divorce Paula because she was the daughter of a *kulak*. She was bringing up her two children alone and wouldn't have been able to take care of me too. I didn't ask as I knew how terribly hard she had to work just to provide for herself and the two children. Most of my other family members had moved away — either forcibly by the communists or through marriage. I was just one of thousands of lost children wandering about on their own. Families had been broken up and everything was in a big mess because of collectivisation.

I walked to the city of Melitopol, begging for food as I went. I boarded a train to Crimea to try to find my sister Frossia. Crimea was a big place with many towns and I had no idea where to look, but I was young and foolish and didn't realise this. I must have been about nine years old by then. I had no ticket and for quite a lot of the way I travelled underneath the train seats. At other times I would travel in boxes that were meant for dogs to travel in on the outside, underneath the carriage of the train. Occasionally I would sit on the roof and sometimes I sat on the outside steps of the train. This was very dangerous as the train was going very fast and could throw up quite large stones.

Finally the train arrived at a small town called Novooleksiyivka, which is known as the gateway to the Crimea. At this station all tickets were checked. The railway police caught me and put me in a children's home — a place they put all the young children they had collected like dogs. They fed us very little and after a couple of days they gave me a dark-coloured flannel shirt. The home was near the railway station so one day when I saw some women selling fried fish to the passengers, I exchanged my shirt for four small fish, which tasted very good. Luckily I still had my undershirt on. The people at the home were trying to send the children back to their families or guardians, if they could find them. They took me back to the council in my village who returned me to Gregory and Tatyana. Of course, he beat me for running away. I started school again and Tatyana helped with my homework, often reading stories to me and telling me to read out loud to help my reading.

CHAPTER III

Feast or famine

BY 1932 food was becoming very short in the villages and many people were moving out to look for food in the towns. It was this year that my sister Paula heard that Tato, Mama and Michael had escaped from the labour camp. Tato and Mama had been digging irrigator ditches, which is extremely heavy work, especially for a woman. They moved from place to place, wherever ditches were needed, finding temporary lodgings at each place. When Paula found them they were living near Zaporizhya, so she moved up there to help them, leaving her two children with her in-laws. Tato had some work and the family was staying at a hostel. Paula managed to get a job but made very little money.

One day my sister Tatyana received a letter from Paula and my parents and told me where they were living. I decided to go to them; I knew it would be better for Tatyana if there was one less mouth to feed. Anyway, I wanted to get away from Gregory. More than anything though, I wanted to see my parents and Michael. So I went north to Zaporizhya by train and as usual, I had no ticket. It was an uneventful journey and eventually I found the place where my parents were staying. Michael was away at school and although Mama and Tato were very happy to see me, food was extremely short.

A couple of days after I arrived, I became very sick with malaria. I was very lucky to be with my family; it's a terrible sickness, especially for a young child. I felt very hot and sweaty one minute, then shivering with cold the next. I couldn't eat a thing. They found a doctor for me and he prescribed quinine, in the form of a powder. The paper it came in was rather thick so someone put it into a cigarette paper and I had to swallow it very quickly. It was very bitter. About four days later my face was very yellow and I was half deaf. I think this was from the medicine. I became so weak that I couldn't walk outside to the toilet. Mother and Paula had to hold me under the arms and help me shuffle to the toilet and back. For about three weeks I was very close to death, and then I slowly began to get better. My appetite returned and I would eat anything they could find for me. The family tried to give me as much food as they could get but there was still a terrible shortage.

During the next few months, as I recovered from my illness, I made friends with a boy called Basil who was eleven years old; about the same age as me. He lived on the other side of the road, not far from us. We would go looking for food and turn it into an adventure.

* * *

One time we managed to find some watermelons and ate some of them; we also ate unripe apricots. One day we climbed a very tall walnut tree and stole some of the unripened nuts. We didn't know that we couldn't eat green walnuts. We stuffed our pockets full and put some down our shirts. Someone saw us and shouted at us. We were quite scared and jumped to the ground. We were very lucky that neither of us was hurt, and ran away as fast as we could, losing half the walnuts on the way. When we felt safe we sat down to rest, and found out soon enough that the nuts we had risked our lives for were not ripe enough to eat. We also found that the brown stains from the green walnuts were badly staining our hands, chests, stomachs and shirts. It was very hard to get off and when we finally arrived home Mama scolded both of us.

My sister, Alexanda, who was unmarried, was living at a hostel in Zaporizhya. We hardly ever saw her. I overheard the family saying that she never helped Mama and Tato in good or bad times, like Tatyana and Paula did. Apparently she had said that she couldn't afford to help, not realising that our parents would have just liked some affection and were not asking for money. The fact that she smoked also seemed to be a mark against her. It was a practice frowned upon by village people, especially for women. I would listen to all the talk and wonder how bad smoking was. I later started smoking myself.

The food shortage was getting worse all the time. Only people who were working were allowed food, which had to be purchased with coupons. I don't know what other food we were allowed to buy, but it was very little. I do remember that each working person was allowed to buy only 400 grams of dark bread a day. My father and Paula were working so we had a little food, but it was not enough to feed four people. My body became very swollen with hunger. I believe my parents gave me most of their food, and after most of the swelling had gone down, I decided to make it easier for my parents and try my luck in the next city. The family were sorry to see me leave again. They appreciated my reason for going and wished me good luck. They said they would pray for me.

* * *

Begging for food along the way, I travelled by train to Dnipropetrovsk, an industrial city about 100 kilometres from Zaporizhya. I wandered around looking for food like a lost dog before coming to a big factory, and finding my way to the factory canteen. I begged for food and picked up scraps from the tables. There wasn't very much food around anywhere but this factory had more food than most places. They had a storeroom for bread, and the caretaker would give me some scraps when he had any to spare. Sometimes the cook gave me food. On the second floor on top of the canteen was a big hall for meetings and a small kiosk with cigarettes and newspapers. Sometimes they held plays and shows and there was a small room behind the stage where the actors could change their clothes. That is where I slept most of the time. The thing that seems to stick in my mind about this place was that on each side of the stage were two large artillery shells.

The factory manager had been told by the top communist of the area that all lost children, whether they were found on the street or in the factory, had to be reported. They would then be sent to a children's home or back to their relatives if they could be found. When I found this out I was horrified, thinking I might have to go back to Gregory. Even if I was sent back to Mama and Tato, they were unable to feed me. I told the manager that my parents had died of hunger and that the children's homes I had been in treated me badly. In fact, I made so much fuss that he felt sorry for me and gave me a job as a messenger in the transport department. I was sent to live in a hostel about three kilometres away. I was a messenger for about two weeks and then they put me in the workshop where they repaired locomotives.

I learnt to be an assistant fitter, helping the other fitters do all sorts of small jobs. There was a nice pendulum clock with a chain in the tool room where I worked and twice I used a broom handle to move the clock hands forward half an hour so I could leave work earlier. The manager caught me the second time and I had to stay half an hour later that day. I would put a bit of oil on my shirtfront to make it look as if I worked harder than I really did. People would say, 'Oh, you're a worker!' when I was walking home and I'd say proudly, 'Yes, yes' as I stuck my chest out.

The factory was very large and had its own enormous railway

yard. The bridge to cross it was far away, and there was so much
rail traffic that people wishing to cross the yard would crawl
under and climb in between the rail wagons. Although everyone
tried to be careful, I heard of quite a lot of accidents. People were
killed or badly injured and one man lost both his legs. I wasn't
working full time and sometimes used the yard as a shortcut, but
not very often.

* * *

I worked five days a week, starting at eight am and finishing at
noon. One day when I was finishing up, the man who worked in
the kiosk selling cigarettes and newspapers asked if I would like to
come to his home for a meal. I was pleased at the thought of food.
I waited until he finished work at four pm, then we walked four
kilometres to his home across the frozen River Dnipro, where he
lived with his elderly mother. They must have felt sorry for me
and decided to invite me over for supper; she had already set a
place for me at the table. We ate borsch and bread, and after the
meal they decided it was too late for me to travel back over the ice,
so invited me to stay the night. I agreed and I got to sleep in a real
bed. In the morning they gave me a breakfast of milk with bread
and a little honey in it. I was very grateful; food was becoming
more and more scarce.

Although I was paid at the factory, it was only a small amount
— enough for food and drink and my living quarters. Sometimes
when I walked home from work, I would see people who had
come from the country looking for food lying on the path in front
of the shops. They were like skeletons and looked almost dead. I
gave them food whenever I had any to spare.

This food shortage was becoming a real famine. Those in the
city who had some work were a little better off and they didn't do

quite as badly as they were given ration cards. In the country, if people went to collective farms they had a little food. If not, the party officials and communist youth took away everything that could be used for food. They even poked and dug the ground in case the people had hidden any food. I heard that many people went mad and ate the bodies of the dead. They were then arrested as that was considered a crime.

The official estimate of the number of people (nearly all Ukrainian) who died in the man-made famine of 1932 to 1933 is seven million; the unofficial count is close to twelve million. This famine was brought about by the communists on Stalin's orders. In Ukraine the man in charge was Lazar Moiseivich Kahanovich, the Jewish second husband of Stalin's sister, who made sure Stalin's orders were carried out as near to the letter as possible. The communist party members, Jews and people from overseas embassies had their own shops and were issued with special cards, which they had to show when they visited these shops. The general Ukrainian population were not allowed to even cross the threshold of these shops. There were also canteens, which catered only for Party members. Very large numbers of the Party were Jewish and a lot of them held high official posts. A large percentage was in the NKVD, which later became known as the KGB. In later years I heard more than once that Ukrainian wheat was offered to Italy at half the usual price. When the Italian authorities said it should go to the starving Ukrainians they were told, 'There is no famine in Ukraine.' Other countries which mentioned it were told the same thing, that it was just false propaganda and there was a surplus, which was why the wheat was sold cheaply.

* * *

One day when I was waiting in a queue of about fifty people to pick up my ration of bread, I saw a piece of wire hanging down at the back of a shop. I was only a young boy and bored, so I thought I'd make myself some glasses out of the wire. I touched it and got a big electrical shock, which knocked me out for a few minutes. I didn't know it was a live wire. Before anyone could come to help me or take my place in the queue I woke up and was all right, but it gave me quite a fright. Some of the other kids laughed because I rolled down a small slope, but they didn't realise that I could have been killed.

Another time I went to the railway station to buy a small amount of food when some teenagers asked me for money for sweets. I told them I only had a small amount of money to buy some biscuits for myself. One of the boys then pushed me and slashed my face with a razor blade he had hidden between his fingers. The razor cut the right side of my face, from my eye to my chin. I didn't feel any pain, only an itch, but when I put my hand to my face I found it covered in blood. My face was bleeding quite profusely and soaking my shirt. I was very frightened. With my hand held tightly to my face, I ran to the first aid post at the railway station, where the sister washed the wound and the doctor put seven metal clips in it. Then the sister put a bandage around my face and head. I went home to the hostel and didn't go to work for about four days. After that I took the bandage off and took the clips out myself and went back to work. I healed quite quickly. Everyone asked me what had happened when I returned to work.

While I was working at the factory, a woman who worked in the transport section of the factory and drove a small locomotive, a type of train with only an engine and no wagons, told the factory management she and her husband would like to foster me, so I went home to live with them. They had two grown-up sons and there was very little room in their house. I slept on the kitchen floor. I stopped working at the factory as they had decided to send me to school. They gave me sandwiches each day for lunch but I was always so hungry that I would eat them on the way to school, long before midday.

Sometimes their sons would play football with me. One day the ball was kicked into the garden next door. I walked in the front gate and up the path to pick up the ball, but as I picked it up a huge German Shepherd dog ran up and bit me on my left leg. I could see lots of blood and puncture marks. I tried to run and the dog started to chase me. I must have made a lot of noise because the owners of the dog came and stopped it. The young men who I had been playing ball with realised that something was wrong and came looking for me. They saw what had happened and carried me home next door. My foster parents cleaned the leg and put a bandage on it.

The family seemed to like me, especially the mother, but just over two months after I went to live with them, she took me back to the factory and left me there. I'm sure I didn't do anything wrong as I liked it there. Perhaps because food was so scarce and they had so little room, they may have decided that they couldn't manage to keep me. But I wished someone had told me why.

A short time later, another couple who also worked in the factory said they would like to foster me. I had been very disappointed when my first foster parents had deserted me, but I thought I might have better luck this time. The couple lived in a small flat and had two small children. I got on very well with the whole family. They would send me for cider and other things from the market, and even though food was scarce they told me to bargain for food and other goods and not to pay the first price asked. One evening I accidentally saw my foster parents lying on the bedroom floor together. I saw nothing else and knew nothing of that side of life. Not knowing any better I told some of my playmates who laughed, although I didn't know why. My foster parents must have heard of this and were very angry with me, shouting and saying that they didn't want the whole area to know what happened in their home. Instead of explaining this quietly and telling me the rules of the house, the next day they took me back to the factory. I had been with them only about two weeks. I had now been deserted by two sets of foster families.

* * *

After that I worked at the factory for about six months but my heart wasn't in it anymore, so I decided to travel by train to Crimea to again try and find my sister. Once again I spent just a few days trying to find her before the police picked me up and took me to a children's home in Feodosiya, a town in Crimea. It wasn't a bad place; it was very close to a picturesque resort area by the sea. There were quite a few sanitariums and holiday resorts for rich people and also for those who were recovering from illnesses and could afford to stay there. I believe it must have been early in 1936 when teenage children of Spanish communists were brought to these holiday homes for safety during the Spanish Civil War. There were about 200 of them. No one from the outside was allowed to go near them, but I could see that they were very good-looking people, especially the girls. Also standing in the bay was a very tall, beautiful four-mast sailing ship called Tovarich, meaning comrade. I liked ships and admired this one. It was a trainee ship for sea cadets.

Feodosiya was the home of a very famous Ukrainian painter, Ivan Aivazovsky. We were free to go into town when we wanted to and some of us visited the art gallery to see his paintings. Even though I was a young boy I knew how good his paintings were. Some of them were very big, from the ceiling to the floor. They were all scenes of the sea and of storms; some were of sailing ships and rocks and others of ships in the harbour. My favourite picture was one of a storm. It was breathtakingly beautiful and I used to enjoy going to have a look at the paintings. Ivan Aivazovsky's tomb and a memorial plaque with a steel fence around it was in the backyard of the children's home and we boys would go behind the tomb to smoke cigarettes.

One day when it was very hot and I was walking by the seaside, I took my shirt off and got very badly sunburnt on the shoulders and back. I have never forgotten it, it was so sore. When the doctor saw my sunburn he said it was quite a bad case and put some white cream on my shoulders and back, telling me to walk only in the shade. I developed very big blisters and it took about four days before I felt even a little better. Most of the time I couldn't be touched or touch anything without great pain. My back was different colours from all this sun burning and I was told I looked like a tiger.

In the town was a big cigarette factory. Now that I was a smoker I liked the smell of the factory. Sometimes people would give us boys from the home a few coins and we would spend the money at the cigarette factory's reject shop where we could buy a few loose cigarettes very cheaply. I stayed about six months at the children's home then travelled by train to Kersch, a commercial fishing port on the point of land that juts out into the channel between Crimea and Kuban.

CHAPTER IV

On the road again

I HAD been wandering around Kersch for a few days when I saw a man coming towards me. I thought I recognised him and he came up to me and said, 'Andrii!' I realised it was my eldest brother, Sidor, whom I had not seen for years. He asked me what on earth I was doing there and I told him everything that had happened to me. He said he was in trouble with the communist authorities and was on the run. He had been in a concentration camp but had escaped and was now a hunted man. We couldn't stay together because he thought it would be too dangerous for me, but we talked for about half an hour. He gave me three rubles and we said goodbye. That was the last time I saw him.

A few days later I saw a few people loading bricks aboard a two-mast sailing boat. I started to talk to them and helped them load the bricks, which they were transporting across the channel to a fishing collective farm company in Kuban. They gave me some food, bread, cheese, salami and plums — people often gave street children food and clothing and they asked me to join them. They liked me and I worked well so they said I could join them in their small fishing company collective. We sailed to a small village in Kuban, Russia, where the skipper of the fishing boat took me to his home for a few days while the boat was being prepared. We then crossed the sea for about 200 nautical miles, taking cargo to villages on the other side of the channel and bringing back building materials. The boat had an engine as well as sails. It was an old engine and had to be warmed up with lamp oil. The fly wheel had to be pushed with a crowbar. Once it was going it was all right, but it was very old fashioned.

One day our boat was standing offshore at anchor when a small motor boat crashed into us. Although there was no damage to either boat, the skipper of the smaller boat swore at us and shouted, 'Why were you in my way?' The whole crew laughed at him thinking it very funny that he had hit a stationary boat, and then had the nerve to rudely blame us. We decided he must be drunk, especially as there were hundreds of nautical miles of open sea and no other boats around. We had fun telling the story to the villagers when we arrived back in port.

When I worked on the fishing boat, I heard that the farming part of the collective had a very good man as manager. He was a Party member — you had to be to obtain such a position — but he was a Ukrainian who had always lived in the Kuban area. I was told that everyone worked well for him, for themselves, and for the good of all. For a collective farm it was well run — too well run for the party officials in Moscow. One year the weather was good and they had very good crops. The farm manager sent the required quota to Moscow and the workers, who were mostly paid with food products, were very well paid that year. Everyone was happy because this meant food for the whole year; enough for the animals, and seeds and grain for sowing next season. But Moscow officials heard about this and were very angry, saying that nearly everything should have been sent to them and that the workers should have been given a lot less. Then they sent the manager to Siberia. Someone else who the workers did not like replaced him. I heard later that the farm never did well again.

* * *

Once when we didn't have very much cargo for the boat, the office clerk of this little fishing place asked me to come with him for company to the next town. We were to travel on horseback to take some papers into the town, about thirty kilometres away. He would stay in town for a few days, as he had work to do, and I was to bring the horses back home. He had a very good horse with a saddle and I had to ride a very rangy old bag of bones with no saddle. He galloped along and I galloped after him, but I became so saddle sore that I was in agony. We arrived in town about midday and took the horses to the public stables where they were fed, watered and rested. We went to the canteen and he bought meals for us both. I had to sit on the edge of the chair because I was so sore. After our meal he said, 'Take the horse and go back to the village.' So I started back straight away.

Because I had both horses I was able to ride the one with the saddle. However, I was so sore I couldn't even sit down on the horse so I had to stand up in the stirrups all the way home. A journey to town travelling both ways took all day, and three quarters of the way back home it became dark and I was quite scared. People had told me there were wolves in the area, so I went as fast as I possibly could. I neither saw nor heard any wolves and arrived back safely.

Back at the fishing village I took the horses to the stable then went to the skipper's house where I lived with him, his wife and two children. They could see how sore I was so I told them what had happened and the skipper gave me some grease to rub on my sore spots. This made me a bit more comfortable, but it still took two weeks before I was healed.

Most of the people in the fishing collective were Ukrainian. The people next door to the skipper's family lent me an old battered book. This was the first time I had read the Kobzar, the book which is almost sacred to Ukrainians. It was written by our greatest poet and patriot, Taras Shevchenko, and I liked the book so much that I cried. There were lots of poems, some that went to the heart of a sensitive person like me. The skipper could see how moved I was and was pleased, telling me I was a "real Ukrainian". I was almost fourteen. I'd had very little schooling but had learnt the basics of reading in my younger years and had taken every opportunity to teach myself to read. However, at the time that I was reading the Kobzar, I hadn't had a chance to read any Ukrainian magazines, books or papers for years.

* * *

Although I was happy at the fishing village and enjoyed the company of the people in the village and the captain and crew, as well as going out on the sea, I only stayed in the fishing village for about two months. By now I was used to travelling and never stayed very long in one place. I decided to travel to the Caspian Sea to try to find my brother, Alexi. I travelled by train, usually hidden in goods trains and sometimes under the seats or on the steps of passenger trains. In fact, anything that was moving in that direction, I would try to get on. I travelled that way for about a week and begged for and stole food and drink when I needed it. I got off the train when it arrived at a very large town called Baku.

I was told by people who knew of my brother that he was living in the next town. So I went there where I met up with a friend of Alexi's who told me that he and Alexi had changed surnames, but kept their first names. The friend's name was similar to ours, Tischenenko, and he said they had exchanged names to protect them both in their new lives. I wanted to find Alexi because I thought that if I was with grown-up members of my family, I would never again have to be at Gregory's mercy. Alexi's friend said that Alexi was in Baku where I had just come from, so I travelled back there and as I then had his address, I was able to find him. When I turned up at his place, I found that he had married a teacher called Maria about a year ago and they had a new baby boy. He had told his wife untruths about his background and family, saying that he was an only child, so he wasn't too happy when I turned up out of the blue. His wife was very understanding when he explained everything to her and she treated me very well, but Alexi was nervous for his family having me there. He also seemed uneasy and perhaps embarrassed at having a street kid for a brother. He didn't want anyone to know he was the son of a farmer because of the way they were treated. He also didn't want to explain why we had different surnames.

* * *

I didn't want to cause any problems for them so I only stayed at their home for two days. I found a job on board a ship as a deckhand. She was a small oil tanker with a crew of about thirty-five men. We were carrying oil from Baku across the Caspian Sea to a small town called Krasnovodsk, meaning "red water" in Central Asia. A strange thing about this town was that they didn't have any fresh water of their own, it was transported to them by train or ship and it was very expensive. It took us three days one way to take our oil to them. Most of the time the weather was good and the crossings uneventful. I enjoyed life aboard the ship, which was called *The Seagull*.

* * *

Once when we were a day out to sea, we received a radio message stating that a "force nine" storm was approaching. The message warned all ships to find a port where they could shelter to wait out the storm. The captain and crew were worried as we were too far out to be able to seek shelter and a force nine storm was a really bad one. Force ten and eleven were hurricanes and twelve was top of the scale and a tornado. We were outward-bound with a full cargo of oil, which was good for ballast. If we had been empty we would have been ripped apart and blown away.

The captain ordered the crew to change course and come around into the wind, which is the only thing to do in such circumstances. Everything was battened down, including the portholes in the cabins. We saw the storm approaching; the clouds were very low and dark and the wind was ripping the water off the sea into the air. It started to get very rough and our poor little boat seemed like a matchbox. On the second day the waves were as high as twelve to fifteen story buildings and were dark green and very scary. It was like climbing up a very high mountain. With every wave that came, we thought it would be the end of us. As we descended on the other side of the wave, it was just as frightening, like going down a ravine. The captain, who had been a seaman for thirty-five years, said he had never seen a storm as bad as this. Some of the crew were very seasick but I wasn't and I was very pleased about that because it was worrying enough just watching the storm rage. Some of the time, from inside the enclosed wheel house, I could see the storm through the large windows. I also spent quite a bit of time in the radio room helping the operator, with whom I got on very well. I could see the storm through those windows too. The storm went on for about four days, after which time it abated slightly.

The sea was still rather heavy, but we were able to come round to our usual course and continue on to our original destination. We had eaten tinned and dried food and drank water while the storm raged, but once it became a little calmer, we were able to do some cooking. From the time we started out from Baku until the time we arrived at our destination, the usual three-day crossing had taken us nine days due to our necessarily roundabout course.

When we arrived at Krasnovodsk, the sea was still heavy so we moved in close to the shore and dropped anchor about one nautical mile out, waiting until the other ships unloaded their cargoes. The sea near the shore was a lot calmer and while we waited to unload our oil, we fished for shrimp with a small net on a piece of string. There were so many of them that within an hour we had a large bucketful. We cooked them with steam and ate so many that we became sick of seeing them. The water was clean and warm and we did a lot of swimming and playing, and jumping and diving from the ship.

* * *

A couple of weeks after the storm, the engineer received a parcel from Ukraine. Some of the items were wrapped in a Ukrainian newspaper. After he'd read the newspaper, he said to me, 'Here, you're Ukrainian, would you like to read this newspaper?' It was a few weeks old but it was wonderful to be able to read a Ukrainian newspaper, and I became a bit teary. Although I got on very well with the crew, the Turkish captain didn't like me much and I wasn't very keen on him either.

CHAPTER V

In the name of defence

I STAYED with the ship for about three months but after that I wanted to travel again, and just wandered around Baku for a while. I was a vagrant, sleeping under steps, in passages and in the railway wagons when they were empty, and

very soon the police picked me up and put me into a children's home again. I worked in the kitchen and as a type of waiter. I hated it, because some of the bigger boys were real hoodlums and were already young criminals. They would strike matches and then stick the lighted match into my arms and shoulders. I only stayed there about a week.

Four boys about my age also decided to leave and so we just walked away as we were not being forced to stay there. We went to the dockside where there was a passenger ship and sneaked on board. We stowed away and hid in a lifeboat, pulling the covers over us. When the ship was more than half a day out to sea, one of the crew discovered us and reported us to the captain. The captain sent us down to the kitchen and put us in the care of the cook, telling him we had to do all the dirty work; scrub and clean everything and peel lots of potatoes. In short, he was to find us as much unpleasant work as possible. The ship's destination was Central Asia and it took us about two and a half days to reach the place we were heading for. We went very near the same port as the oil tanker I had been on, but this was a faster ship.

When we reached the ship's destination, it turned out to be a very small settlement and behind it was nothing but desert. No trees or other vegetation at all, only sand. There was absolutely nothing else there except a few huts with one or two people. The ship anchored close to the shore, and after they unloaded their paying passengers they took us five boys in a small boat and just dumped us on shore. It was a very bad place to be stranded because if we wanted to continue our travels, there was hardly anywhere that we could go. We needed to get into the next town where we were told by one of the men that there was a railway station.

* * *

It was eighty kilometres across the desert to the next town and it was already quite late in the evening. It was not the sort of journey we could make on foot and we didn't know what to do. We spied a three-tonne truck containing a few boxes and four Arabs sitting in the back, so we asked the Russian driver for a lift. He said no and started to drive away, but I ran very quickly and caught the back of the truck, pulling myself up. The Arabs in the back did not help me but did not try to stop me either. After I managed to climb aboard I squeezed in between two boxes. The other boys were left behind; they hadn't acted quickly enough to jump on board. I don't know what happened to them.

One of the boxes I was sitting next to was partly opened and I could see that it contained biscuits. I was very hungry so I ate some. After a couple of kilometres, the driver stopped to see if everything was all right, because the road was very bumpy. He saw me and said in Russian, 'So you managed to get on.' He let me stay on board and I was very glad he didn't make me get off because we were a fair way into the desert by this time. When we arrived at the next town it was already night time and quite dark. The Arabs and the Russian driver went their different ways. I knew there was a railway station there so I made enquiries and found out where it was. I walked down to the station and decided to stay there for the night. I slept on the seat in the station and I had been asleep for about half an hour when a policeman came along and woke me up. He took me to the police station and the next day the authorities put me in a children's home again.

* * *

This children's home, which was in Krasnovodsk, was not bad as children's homes go. The weather was nice and warm in Central Asia and we children could walk into town and play on the beach and the rocks. Outside the town was the desert, but we didn't go there. One thing that I really hated about that children's home was the smell of the sewerage. It would go into a huge tank and at night people would come and empty the tank into trucks to be taken away. The smell was very bad indeed. I remember a little while after I arrived at the children's home that I had a very bad infection in my ears. It was very painful and I felt like banging my head on the wall. I thought I was going to go crazy with the pain. They gave me some medicine but it didn't ease the pain. However, it only lasted three days and then it cleared up completely.

Krasnovodsk was the town with no water, which I had visited during my time with the fishing collective. Huge tanks of water had to be brought in by ship and train. The tanks would then be connected to pipes with taps, which were housed in two small brick buildings. Two women would sit in the buildings, one in each place, and if someone needed fresh water they had to go in and pay the women who would turn on the tap. The water was very expensive. Eleven kopeks for a medium bucketful and two kopeks for a cupful. You could bring your own cup, but for people who didn't have one with them, everyone had to drink from the same cup which was on a chain.

The children's home had a big tank for water, which was also brought in by ship and train. I stayed at this home for about two months before an official appeared making enquiries about which of the Ukrainian children could be sent back to their relatives. They took all the Ukrainian children together on a ship to Baku where they had a special centre for lost children. I was afraid, because I thought they might send me back to Gregory. I didn't want to go back to him, so I just walked away.

* * *

I looked around Baku for two or three days; I had been there before, but this time I saw a big building for the Communist Youth Organisation so thought I would make use of them. I went inside and asked if they could get me a job. They said, 'Yes, we would be very pleased to get you a job and we will help you, but you will have to join our organisation a little later.' I let them think that I would do so but I had absolutely no intention whatsoever of joining any communist organisation. I was only thinking of my present situation, hoping I could find a job and let the future run its course. They gave me a form to fill out and sign but I said I would fill it out later. I kept putting it off or pretending I had forgotten. I never did sign it.

They took me to a factory and I was taken on as an apprentice assistant fitter in the tool room. I was pleased that this factory did not belong to the Communist Youth Organisation and that I would not be working for them. I was shown where I would sleep. It was like a small dormitory, with five beds used by the single boys who worked there. It was on the second floor and the big boss lived on the first floor. This boss had a son named Victor who was my age — about fourteen — and he and I became very good friends. One day we were playing on a path near the road.

I was throwing a coin up into the air and he was trying to grab it. I spun around quickly and must have stepped onto the road. I threw my arm up and didn't see a small lorry headed towards me. I hit the lorry's headlight with my hand and the mudguard caught me and threw me onto the road. Thankfully I was not run over. The driver stopped and he and Victor and a few other people took me to the clinic directly across the road. Everyone was making a big fuss and talking at once and asking what happened. Although I had quite a big piece of glass in my thumb, a few minor bumps and grazes and a very big fright, I wasn't badly injured. The clinic fixed me up and I was given four days off with pay. If I had stepped out a little further, I could have been run over and killed.

When I had started work at the factory, all the workers were told we could "volunteer" to give a quarter of our monthly wages to the Central Government in Moscow for four months. We also had to give money to help the communists in Spain who were fighting against General Franco. It was called volunteering, but you could not refuse unless you wanted to be called a traitor, because the "borrowed" money was supposedly for defence. This system was also called a "lottery" and we were each given a ticket which they said could win us a car or 100,000 rubles. Nobody had ever heard of anyone winning.

Once when I ran out of money, I went to the bank to see if I could get some money for my ticket. I received three rubles even though it had cost me about 180 rubles, but it was better than nothing. I knew I had no chance of winning any lottery.

Every month a man carrying a sackful of money and escorted by an armed guard would come to the factory. They took the money from the sack, put it onto the table and counted out the money for each person, according to the list he carried. We would queue up, our names would be called and we would sign

for our money, less the "defence lottery" and Spanish communists' money which would have already been deducted. We had
to queue up for just about everything. The old woman cook at the
canteen would let me eat and pay her after I received my wages.
The meal gong was a train bumper plate hung just inside the factory door. Someone would bang it with a piece of steel when it
was time to eat. After paying for my living quarters and food, I
had very little left. I was almost fourteen years old at this time and
never seemed to have any money. Two girls about my age took
me to a film in the business area of Baku and they also bought
me some sweets.

* * *

Baku is quite a large city and is the capital of Azerbaijan. There
were two distinct areas of Baku, one called Black Town, the
industrial area, the other called White Town, the business area.
I lived in the Black area. Our factory was very near an oil refinery,
which made a lot of pollution and a lot of very dark, dirty yellow
smoke which killed all the flies. There was also a railway line
close by, where the trains brought the oil to the refinery. The
trains themselves made quite a lot of smoke and lots of oil was
dropped. It seemed to be everywhere, including the paths, so
we had to walk in pollution all the time, but nobody seemed to
be concerned.

One day a few of us boys went by electric train to the airfield
on the outskirts of the city to see the arrival of an airship. We had
never seen an airship before, so it was quite a big event. There
was a big tower and the airship was tied to it. The people stepped
from the airship onto the tower steps and then came down the
tower. We saw it from a short distance away. It was like a huge,
long, silver balloon. I thought it was beautiful and would have

loved to have had a ride on it. However, airship tickets were very expensive and I couldn't afford anything like that. It wasn't possible to stow away on a dirigible.

Another day I was sitting on the balcony of my room after work reading a comic and watching the traffic when I saw a fire engine. It was not rushing to a fire and the firemen were wearing their best brass helmets and smart uniforms. I think they were going to an inspection or a parade. Behind them the fire chief rode in a long, sleek, shiny red open car. It was maroon red, not bright red like the fire engine. I had never seen a car like it before and thought it was beautiful. When I spoke about it later, someone told me it was called a Lincoln, which they said was a very expensive type of car.

I can remember walking along a path, window shopping in the White area of Baku, when I saw four very small people. I thought how very well dressed they were for children but when I looked at their faces, I could see that they were older people. There were two men and two women. I had never seen such small adult people before and was very surprised. They were perfectly formed but so small! I was told later that they were midgets, or small people, and were theatre actors. I admired their clothing, especially their leather coats and fine felt hats.

* * *

I was in Baku for May Day 1936, the day the communists had their big celebrations and demonstration. We all had to gather at our workplace wearing our best clothes and the factory's political organiser made sure we were all there. Party members had prepared placards, flags and portraits of communist leaders for us to carry. We had to line up five abreast on the road outside our factory. I didn't have to carry anything because I was too small. I hated it all, but couldn't get out of it. We had no say; we knew we had to march and that was that. On our way to the big square, we were joined by marching groups from other factories. There were also bands playing patriotic Soviet communist music.

When we arrived the cavalry was already lined up. The men were very smart in their uniforms and they had really beautiful horses. There were about a dozen small short-barrelled cannons each pulled by four horses. Behind them were fifteen two-horse carriages, each carrying a heavy machine gun. On each carriage, two men sat with the gun and another with the horses. I remember one of the cavalry horses going wild, jumping and kicking and trying to run away. Maybe it was an anti-communist like me! After a while, the rider managed to calm it down. The horses were beautifully groomed. Most people looked after their horses very well, especially the army cavalry units.

On the dais were about a dozen important communist leaders who watched as we marched past them. I was surprised to see a very tall black man standing with them. I had never seen a Negro before, but I had heard about them. I didn't know who he was at the time, but later we were told that he was Paul Robson, the American singer. I never knew for sure if it was him, but that was the rumour. He was there as a special guest of honour. After the parade, some people took the red flags, banners, placards, large photos of communist leaders and other bits and pieces back to the factories and everyone was allowed to go home and take the rest of the day off.

At the time of the May Day celebrations I had been at that factory in Baku for about five months, a long time for me in those days, so I decided to move on. One day I packed a few clothes and some food in a small suitcase and told the people that I was leaving. They said they had hoped I would stay, and asked why I was going. I told them I was homesick and wanted to travel home to Ukraine.

CHAPTER VI

Collective concentration

I RODE the trains again and after I had travelled for about two days, someone stole my suitcase while I was asleep. Now I had nothing except a small amount of money, which I carried on me. The ticket I had bought was only for a short distance, just enough to get on the train. Travelling by train was very expensive, especially for me, so by this time I was travelling with no ticket. The train arrived in Ukrainian territory and at one station, ticket inspectors boarded the train and caught me. They took me to the Railway Police, who arrested me and took me to the police station at Mariupol. They put me in a cell for the night. It was nearing the end of 1936 and I was not yet fourteen years old. By the next morning I was taken with about twenty other people to a large prison where I was put in a very small room absolutely packed with people. It was so crowded we couldn't breathe and people started collapsing. When the prison wardens realised this they put us all in a room which was a bit bigger. However, we only had enough room to lay down on the very cold floor and when anyone moved, we all had to move.

We were on the second level of the prison which seemed to have five or six storys. In this tiny room near the door, was a small barrel used as a toilet which was emptied once a day. A small window was partly covered with wood on the outside so that the people inside could only see a small patch of sky. We were given 400 grams of black bread a day. In the mornings we were given half a cup of warm brown liquid which they called tea, but tasted like warmish water, and in the evenings terrible soup made of

51

fish heads and other rubbish. On my family's farm we had given better food to our pigs.

I was kept in this room for just over two weeks. Some people had been in the prison a lot longer and were allowed parcels from home. Being a very small room, everyone tried to move in a way that was most beneficial to all and the people receiving parcels would share with the others. I was told that there was a law among prisoners, that if anyone stole another person's ration of bread he would be killed.

After a couple of weeks a group of us and a group from another cell were taken to a court room. One at a time we went through a door and stood in front of a table at which three NKVD officers were seated. When my turn came they asked my name, where I was born and what crime I had committed. Then I was taken out another door into the prison courtyard, where about 100 people were standing. In one hour, they had all been through the court, if you could call that place a court. We stood around for a while, then an official came and read out a list of the crimes and sentences of each person.

* * *

Political crimes were dealt with very severely. If a person said one word against the government, the system or any political leader, they could be sentenced to twenty-five years in a labour camp in Siberia. They could even be shot, depending on what had been said. I heard that children as young as twelve could be shot for speaking up against the government. One woman was given seven years for selling eggs in the market, and they denounced her as a speculator. Someone who had left their collective farm for the city without permission was given five years. (People often did this and didn't usually get caught, but a pass was supposed to be carried at all times.) I was sentenced to three years in a concentration camp for riding on a train with no ticket.

I was taken, along with twenty other young people, to a concentration camp outside the city of Meriupol. When we arrived we were assigned beds, the double story type. We were given a mattress and two thin blankets. Not everyone was taken to the same camp. I was told people with long sentences were often sent to Siberia or other equally cold and desolate places. Apparently the communists needed labourers and used any excuse to give people long sentences so that they had slaves working for next to nothing under appalling conditions.

The next day eighteen of us were taken out to work. The leader of our band was a young German man. We marched to the gate, then a guard was assigned to escort us to a military factory where we had to shovel coke and coal on to railway wagons. It was a very big factory which had its own railway line running inside it. It was very heavy work because as well as shoveling the coal, we had to carry cast iron, iron ore and other heavy metals and load them onto the rail trucks. If the metal was very heavy, two young men would have to carry it on a homemade stretcher. This was terribly hard work for a very young boy. We had to repair and replace the rail tracks and bumpers and did all the work necessary to keep the railway running smoothly for the factory. In winter, we had to move any ice that had formed on the railway tracks. We had to carry wooden sleepers and metal train rails to make new lines. Two of us would carry the extremely heavy sleepers on our shoulders. When carrying the rails we would use special metal claws to grip them. Our group of eighteen would then carry the rails between us, nine on each side. This was also very heavy work.

Our main guard inside the factory was a Ukrainian man who treated us quite well. He would speak to us in Ukrainian and sometimes crack jokes. We worked ten hours a day, six days a week. If we worked well, the management of the factory would tell our camp authorities and we would be given a little more food. The name of the band who had worked well would be written up on a board in the canteen. We were given thirty rubles at the end of each month which was very little money. To compare how much it was, a litre of vodka cost twelve rubles, a kilo of butter twenty-four rubles and a kilo of bacon twenty-two rubles. The other factory workers were all free men and would sometimes give us food such as soft white bread, cheese, salami, milk and also cigarettes. The factory management didn't stop them. We were all young hard-working boys who didn't get enough to eat in the camp. Even the factory management who knew we were not criminals would see that we got extra food. The type of food they gave us seemed so luxurious after the camp food.

I was released from the camp sometime around the end of 1937. I was told that as a good worker, I was being allowed what was called a one for three. They said the reduction meant that for every three days I should have served I had served only one, making it one year instead of three. However, I read later in the newspapers that many courts had been closed and new ones set up because thousands of people had been sent to jails and camps for no good reason. The men running these courts were now called enemies of the people. Some had been sacked, others shot. A person's fortune could change very quickly under the communists. It seems that these changes to the court system were happening all over the country, although I had my doubts about whether things would be much better.

* * *

When they freed me I was given a small amount of money, enough for about two days, but I soon found a job in the same town, Mariupol. I could have had a job as a free man at the factory I had been working at but decided against it. I found lodgings at a hostel and walked three kilometres to and from work each day. My new factory was a smelter for steel and other metals, and also made coke out of coal. This was the part I worked in. It was very hot work and the fumes were rather overpowering, giving off a terrible stench. A special wagon would be loaded with hot coal by a machine, which would then push the wagon into a specially fortified tower so it could be showered with water. The machine would close the door and I had to walk on a high platform quite close to the furnace to see if the door was properly closed and that no steam was escaping. Because my job was hot and I breathed a lot of fumes, the factory gave me a free litre of milk, a little butter and sugar and 400 grams of bread each day. This had to be consumed on the premises.

I worked there for about six months and then left because it was too hot and I was fed up with the job. I also felt that, in a strange way, I was being drawn back to my own village. I thought I would try to go back and see if there was anyone I knew still living there. I travelled from Mariupol to Melitopil by bus and then walked the forty kilometres to my village of Stepanivka. I went to my sister Tatyana's house and found that she was very pleased to see me. I was still a bit scared of her husband but, as I had grown up quite a lot, I hoped he would leave me alone. He totally ignored me. I stayed there two days then moved on because I wanted to find Mama and Tato. Tatyana told me that Mother, Father and Michael were living in a village called Terpenia, so I decided I would walk there to see them.

I started walking the forty kilometres back to Melitopil and along the way managed to get a job on a small farm, doing any work that needed to be done. There were large orchards with many different kinds of fruits, but I enjoyed picking pears the most because they were the most beautiful pears I had ever seen. They were half-yellow and half-red and so big and juicy that if they were left on the trees too long they would fall off and squash flat on impact. Sometimes I would cut watermelons and lift them on to trucks to be taken to the city. I also worked with the horses, a job I liked. The horses would pull a small cultivator for clearing grass.

One day when I was going for my midday meal, I was walking along a small path through the pear orchard when a small, black, very poisonous snake slithered close to my feet. I was very frightened and struck it with a small horse crop I was carrying. I hit it a couple of times and managed to kill it. I considered myself very lucky as these snakes could strike swiftly — they don't try to keep out of the way of humans, as other snakes do. I walked along after that, swishing away flies with the crop as I had been doing before, trying to tell myself I hadn't really been frightened. After I calmed down I went and had my meal.

* * *

I stayed at the farm for about two months, long enough to save a small amount of money because I didn't want to arrive at my parents' place broke. I then completed my journey to Melitopol and walked eighteen kilometres to the village of Terpenia, where my family was living. They were very surprised and pleased to see me. They were living in a small flat and my sister, Frossia, who had been a nanny in Crimea, was also with them. We talked and talked and Frossia told me she had travelled around a lot, as I had, and that she had also had a few adventures. Michael wasn't there; he was away at school. He was going to be a tradesman and was learning to make fireproof bricks. He boarded at the school which was in the large city of Zaporizhya. I was told that he would also learn other trades later.

Mama, Tato and Frossia had no choice but to work on a collective farm. Mama looked after the household duties and the garden, while Tato took care of the collective farm's horses. He nearly always had this job because he was so good with them. Frossia and the other young girls looked after silkworms in an enormous shed. They collected the branches from mulberry trees and laid them out on shelves so the silkworms could eat the leaves. The cocoons from the silkworms were taken to a factory and made into silk, and each year Frossia and the other girls would be given a few metres of first grade silk as a bonus because they worked so well. They could only do this job at a certain time of the year and the rest of the time they would work in the fields and pick ripe fruit from the orchards.

After working for one year on a collective farm, the head of a household would be given half an acre of land to build a mudbrick house, sheds and whatever other buildings were needed. The families were then trapped — that was part of the government's plan. People had no choice but to work on the collective farms because there was no other work to be had in the country areas. When I arrived, my family had been at the collective farm just over a year and had already started to build a house on the land allotted to them. I lived in the flat with my family and helped build the house whenever we had time away from our other work. Everyone in the family helped, even Mama who was a very hard worker. It was very hard work for all of us.

I was pleased to be back with my parents and Frossia. I spent most of my time helping to finish the house and working on the collective farm. Sometimes I even had some spare time to play football. My mother, Frossia and I took turns standing in queues outside shops, especially if we needed material. The shopkeepers would tell the villagers beforehand if they were expecting materials or other products then, depending on what we needed, I would arrive at the shop very early in the morning. There would always be people waiting when I arrived, having stood or sat outside the shop all night. I would stand for between two and three hours, talking and listening to other people in the queue, until Frossia had finished her chores and could relieve me. After Frossia had stood there for a few hours, Mama would relieve her.

Often, despite our great need, it was not worth the wait. The shops were government-owned, and were used as dumping grounds for unwanted supplies. Many people were forced to buy items they didn't want just so they could buy what they needed. For example, if a person wanted kerosene they also had to purchase a two kilogram bag of nails. Or, if they wanted cotton for the sewing machine, they had to buy after-shave lotion, which most country people didn't use and couldn't really afford.

Unfortunately for us all, the top communist officials of the village, their relatives and good friends would sneak in the back doors of the shops and buy the very best of whatever the shop sold, especially materials. They never had to stand in queues. Sometimes, after waiting all day, we would find that there was nothing left when we finally reached the counter. The communists had taken it all.

* * *

We finally finished building our house. It was quite small, with one room and a large corridor, which was also used as a storage area. It couldn't compare to our original farmhouse, which was quite large. We also had a shed at the side of the new house and we had one cow, one she-goat with two kids, a few pigs, half a dozen chickens and a small dog. Although we had very little money, we scraped and saved and bought young animals to build up our livestock. These animals belonged to us, not the collective farm, but each year every family had to pay taxes in the form of produce. Officials would visit each family and decide how much milk and eggs had to be given in accordance with how many animals each family owned. Every family also had to give forty kilograms of meat each year. To prevent too many animals being killed to pay the taxes, our family and four others pooled our money and bought a young cow. This animal was presented alive to the officials as the five families' meat tax for that year. The cow was accepted and led away to a waiting truck.

We had a small cart on two wheels which my father and I would pull ourselves. In autumn we would go into the fields and collect all the tumbleweeds that had blown everywhere. It was in round balls, like the tumbleweeds you see in American films set in ghost towns. It had collected on the fences and everywhere else and we would have to scoop it up with pitchforks because it was very prickly. We used it on our fires instead of coal or wood. We also had a garden and the soil was very fertile. Mother would look after the garden; she liked gardening and had always done that sort of work. She would plant vegetables and sometimes a few flowers.

Every morning the workers would walk to the collective farm and the overseer would tell us where we were working that day. Father's job was nearly always with the horses while everyone else had a variety of jobs. I worked in the fields or orchards, wherever I was told to work. There were many different fruit trees in the orchards and I didn't mind fruit picking because we were allowed to eat the fruit as we picked. A lot of the trees had cherries, which were my favourite fruit. Not many people liked working on the collective farms, not that they had any choice. However, because all the farming families were working on the collectives the famine had ended.

Since prehistoric times, since people first tilled the soil and planted crops, farmers have worked with nature. However, after the communists started collectivisation, the farmers had no say in the running of the farms. They had become slaves and had to do as the Party officials told them. These officials were from towns and knew nothing of farming but still everyone had to obey them. Many things were done incorrectly, against the climate, the type of soil and the natural order of growing things. If anyone spoke up, the overseers would say that the instructions came straight from Moscow and were Party policy. The Party couldn't make mistakes, so woe betide anyone wanting to question orders! On one farm, the workers were told to sow 2000 acres of wheat in an area where the soil was unsuitable and should have been left fallow that year. But the farmers would be told how much wheat or other produce had to go to Moscow and any shortfall had to be made up with something else. Under normal circumstances, grain and seed would be saved for next year's planting and also as food for the workers and animals, but the Soviet government didn't worry about that; they had to have their quota.

* * *

On this farm we could bring our own lunch or go home to eat. I usually went home. One day in the summertime, most of the younger people were working in the orchards and when lunchtime came around, I decided to go home. I don't know how, I must have been daydreaming, but I got onto a wrong path. I walked and walked, hoping I would see something familiar, until after a while I came to a river and realised I was lost. I came upon an enormous rock, which was like two or three rocks together and as large as three or four houses. It was like a small mountain. I had seen this rock before but only from a distance. There was also a small market garden there, irrigated by the river. I was told later that this was a very famous rock where archaeologists had found artefacts such as jewellery, ornaments, crockery and bones from prehistoric times. It was an ancient burial place and was called the rock grave. (Many years later, I read about this famous rock in a book and saw pictures of some of the artefacts. There was a very large piece of gold with embossed figures on it. It had been the breastplate of a warrior who had been buried wearing it. The book said this and the other treasures dated from the 4th Century BC.) After a while, I figured out where I was and, as I have always had a good sense of direction, I followed the river and in time found my way home.

* * *

We were all working in the fields one day near a shed where people who didn't go home could eat their meals, when party officials arrived with a film crew and the head of the collective farm. They had two lorries, one carrying a large movie camera and other equipment and the other carrying enormous round mirrors made of silver paper instead of glass. The officials told the farm boss what they wanted and he ordered us to bring everything they would need to make the film. He then supervised while we brought everything out from the farm stores. We put out a long table and covered it with a white tablecloth and then brought bread, cakes, fruit and many other foods as well as tall glasses, bottles of wine and vases of flowers. While we were doing this, the officials had picked five of the prettiest girls, my sister Frossia among them, and drove them back to the village so they could put on their very best clothes. The officials sat at the table and when the girls came back, they were told to act as if they were waitresses. Everyone was told to put on big smiles. They were false smiles of course. This was a propaganda film. All the men and boys had to stand to one side, near the shed. I moved back as far as I could but I could still see what was happening. The light was poor but they used bright lights and made lots of photographs for this movie. As soon as the filming was finished, the crew packed up their equipment and off they all went. We were ordered to quickly put all the food and other props away. Of course, we were not allowed any of these luxuries. I saw a very small part of this film with other snippets many years later, but I didn't get a good look as it was gone too quickly.

* * *

Later that year, outside the village, I was walking along a road with a few other young men. The sky was very clear except for one small cloud. We saw something that looked like a long tube come out of the cloud and meet up with dust from the field. It became a small whirlwind. We saw this from a short distance away but it didn't cross our path and we could hear the swish and swoosh as it passed. It travelled for about three kilometres and then just dissolved. We had seen a small lorry travelling towards us, and when the people in the lorry saw the whirlwind they stopped a short distance from us. There were five men on board who must have been some sort of film crew — we saw one of them cranking the handle of a camera and following the course of the whirlwind. These people were not the film people who had taken the pictures at the collective farm.

We all went to look at the path of destruction the whirlwind had made. The grass and sweetcorn was totally flat where it had passed, as if a giant roller had been passed over it. The ground was littered with dead birds, and all sorts of debris and dust were scattered everywhere. We were glad that it had cut across the sweetcorn field and had not come our way, as we would not have had time to get away.

CHAPTER VII

Travelling full circle

A T THE end of 1939 I had been back with my parents for
about a year and a half. I was seventeen and although I had
thought that all I wanted was to be with my family, the collective farm was just like slavery and I was used to travelling about.
I told my parents that I would like to try and get a job in the city.
They were sorry to see me go but said it was up to me; they knew
that I could look after myself after all the travelling I had done.

I told my good friend, Basil, and he decided to go with me.
Young people had a better chance of getting away from collective farms than adults and we were very careful not to get caught.
We walked until we came to a railway line where we saw a goods
train. We sneaked on board and hid in a closed wagon containing only a few boxes. The boxes were tightly closed and we did
not touch them and in a very short time we were on our way. We
travelled on this train until we came to a town called Kherson, on
the banks of the River Dnipro — my country's largest and most
famous river. We got off the train and walked along the riverbank.

We saw three lorries full of watermelons parked on the pier
ready to be loaded onto a river barge. Both Basil and I liked
watermelons, so I said to the eldest man there, 'Will you give
us a watermelon?' He replied, 'Yes, if you will help us load the
watermelons onto the barge.' These watermelons were about the
size of footballs and not very heavy. We helped three men load all
the watermelons and when we had finished the older man, who I
think was a foreman, told us we could have as many watermelons

as we liked. We told him we could only manage one, so he gave us five rubles each as well. Although this wasn't very much money, it was more than we had expected. We thanked him and when the men had left, we sat on the bank of the river and ate part of the watermelon, cutting it up with our pocketknives. We then rolled a cigarette each and smoked them.

Further along the riverbank we found an upturned boat. When dusk started to fall we crawled under it and lay down, but the mosquitoes were so bad that we could not sleep. We got up and collected dry cowpats and made a fire, hoping the smoke would chase the mosquitoes away (and being smokers, we always carried matches). But it only helped a little and we did not get very much sleep that night. In the morning the mosquitoes left us and we managed to get some sleep at last. We slept quite late, until about half past nine. The fire had gone out but it was a warm day. We had brought some food with us in linen bags. I had bread, a piece of cooked bacon and some dried fruit. Basil had brought bread and cheese. We shared this food and finished the watermelon. We also drank water from the river, because although the melon was very juicy it was also very sweet.

After breakfast we decided to cross the river, so we borrowed the boat. It was a light rowing boat and we had no trouble moving it. Basil said he couldn't row, but it was such a small craft that I knew I would have no trouble managing it. When we got to the water's edge I told Basil to jump in so that I could push the boat out into the water. I jumped in, rowed a short way out and then got a shock. I looked down at some bright red water in the bottom of the boat and realised I had a deep gash on my right toe. We never wore shoes in summer and I must have stepped on some broken glass, but the water was so cold I had felt no pain. I needed medical treatment and as we were only a short way from shore, I rowed back to the place we had just left.

Once on dry land, I tied my hankie around my toe and we pulled the boat on to the bank. About 200 metres away we could see houses and a medical clinic and Basil helped me hobble over. Ukrainian clinics were open 24 hours a day. There were people already waiting there, but when they saw I was bleeding they let me go first. The doctor gave me an injection, cleaned the wound, put five clips in it and bandaged it up. I did not have to pay for my treatment, because doctors and other health workers at that time received a set wage, which was decided upon and paid for by the government. After I had thanked the doctor we left the clinic and slowly walked into Kherson, which was a large town even in those days.

We saw a large restaurant and went around to the kitchen to ask if they had any leftover food we could have. One of the cooks gave us some bread and a plate of milk pudding each. We were told to eat it outside in the back alley. After we had given the plates and spoons back and thanked the staff, we walked to a large park where we rested for a long time because my foot had become very painful. When it grew darker, we again went down to the riverside. This time we found a bigger boat which only had nets and other fishing gear onboard. This boat had a cabin and a door we could close and we found that we had a lot less trouble with mosquitoes.

* * *

We wandered around Kherson for three days going to different restaurants and cafes begging for food. We were always given something to eat and drink. We also slept in the same fishing boat by the river each night. My toe was quite painful for a while but it seemed to be healing all right, so after three days I took the clips out and threw them and the bandages in a litter bin and we decided to look for a job. We went to the rail yard just outside town and asked a foreman if there was any casual work we could do. We were told we could have two days' work stacking boxes on pallets if we wanted it. We accepted. They were medium-size boxes and we had no idea what was in them as the box labels only had numbers on them, but they were not very heavy, only about ten kilograms each.

It was summertime, but not very hot, and it was daylight until early evening, so we worked ten hours a day. We still slept onboard the beached boat. We considered it a good job and we were given enough time for meal breaks. There was a canteen and although the other workers paid for their meals, the foreman told the kitchen staff to give us any food they could spare. We were given good food, such as borsch or mashed potatoes, and also rice pudding and other milk puddings. They also gave us some apples to take away with us.

At the end of two days we were given seventy-five rubles each. Even though we had worked very well and for long hours, we considered seventy-five rubles each good money for two days' work. After our job finished we said goodbye and thanked the foreman and workers and walked back into Kherson. We thought the five days we had spent there was enough, so we decided to travel to Crimea. Although we had money now we didn't know how long it would have to last, so once again we sneaked aboard a goods train and hid in an empty closed wagon.

We talked as we travelled and I said that I intended to continue on. Basil told me he had been trying to decide if he should go on with me or go back home. As the train drew in to the station at Melitopol, he told me that he had changed his mind about coming with me and was going home. He said he would have to go now as it would be much easier for him to return home from Melitopil than if he travelled further towards Crimea. I was sorry to lose his companionship but it was his decision, so we said goodbye and good luck. Although I never saw Basil again, a few years later I heard that he had arrived home safely and that later he and his family had moved to another village.

* * *

After Basil left, I travelled for about 100 kilometres until the train stopped at a station called Dzhankoi, in Crimea. It was a junction and the end of the line for this train so I sneaked off. There were only a few houses there, so I decided to go over to the platform where passenger trains left for Simferopol. Although I had money, I wasn't sure how long it would last so I bought a ticket for half the journey, just to get on to the platform. The tickets of passengers leaving or boarding trains were not checked at stations in those days. The only danger was the ticket inspectors, who were often onboard. This time, however, I managed to travel all the way to Simferopol without being caught.

When I arrived I found there were no railway lines to Yalta, a small town in Crimea, and I would have to travel by bus. I wasn't sure if I wanted to go straight to Yalta or stop along the way, so again I bought a ticket for half the journey. As the bus approached the halfway mark, I had to either leave the bus or pay the rest of the fare. I looked out of the window and saw a small village. I needed food, drink and somewhere to sleep and decided to continue my journey to Yalta later. Getting off the bus I walked over to a collective farm and asked a few people walking along the street where the farm office was. I was shown to a large building and went over and asked for a job. They were very pleased to have an extra worker and said I could start in the morning picking tomatoes. I was told that I could sleep in the stable and was given some bread and milk.

Some people may not like the thought of sleeping in a stable, but I've always found it very pleasant. The stable was very large and there were about twenty horses. The groom slept in his area of the stable. It was clean and the hay was warm and dry and I liked the smell and company of the horses. In the morning I was told I could go to the kitchen for breakfast where I was given tea, bread and jam. Although the people who worked permanently on the collective had their own dwellings, there was a kitchen to cater for casual workers. After breakfast, I went with ten other workers to the fields and picked tomatoes. We put them in baskets and later packed them in boxes and stacked them. This job lasted two days and I was given nearly fifty rubles. This was good money. Although people on collective farms did not live very well, casual workers received good money and were welcome if they arrived when fruit or vegetables needed gathering.

After leaving the farm I started to walk towards the small sea port of Yalta. I had only walked about two kilometres when a small farm lorry carrying bags of potatoes and beetroot pulled up and the driver offered me a lift. He wasn't going all the way into Yalta but he took me to the outskirts. I thanked him and walked the last few kilometres. Although I tried at many places, I couldn't get a job anywhere, so I decided to leave Yalta immediately and walk the eighteen kilometres to the next town, a small place called Simeiz. Between these two places was a very beautiful area with wonderful scenery and lots of holiday homes. There were also beautiful old mansions where the Russian Czars, their families, other royalty and their nobility would visit in the olden days for holidays, and which were still used as holiday homes by the Soviet communist elite.

* * *

In Simeiz I managed to get a job as a kitchen hand at a holiday resort. I was told I would be given a three-day trial period. For the three days I was allowed to sleep in the boiler house, which was quite large. I slept on a wooden bench in my clothes. I needed no bedding because it was comfortably warm in there. When the three days were up I was told I had worked well and the job was mine. I was then allowed to sleep in a large dormitory with five other men. Some of the workers gave me a shirt, trousers and a pair of sandals, as I was still barefoot.

Army officers from the Kiev military district region came to the resort with their families for holidays and there were enormous amounts of food and wine about, a lot of which was wasted. I wasn't used to this and I was very shocked by the waste after I had been so hungry myself and seen so many people starve to death. After I mentioned this wastage I was told that instead of throwing leftovers away I could give them to the doormen, the gatekeepers, gardeners and any other workers. It was sinful that so much food was wasted when people were still hungry, although the famine was now over. It was ridiculous. Dozens of rissoles would be rejected just because they were a little too brown, or the rice pudding might be a little too thick, or the eggs not perfectly cooked. I was disgusted and I wasn't the only one who thought like that. Everything had to be fresh each day. It had to be used that day or discarded and it would have been impossible for the officers' families to eat all the food that was brought in. Sometimes there were only forty families and we were expected to use a twelve kilogram box of butter in one day. The guests would have five meals a day. Breakfast, second breakfast, lunch, afternoon tea and supper and if they wanted more food after that, they could have it.

My first job in the morning was to clean, lay and light the big wood stove. We were only allowed to use wood; no other fuel was used as they believed food tasted better when cooked on a wood stove. I helped the cook and did lots of jobs like chopping and mincing meat, chopping up vegetables, stirring soup and milk and seeing that the fire did not go out. I got on very well with the cook, who loved to drink Madeira wine, and I would often go to the shops just to collect the Madeira for him. The man who had the job before was older than me and had been called up into the army when the Soviet Union had tried to take Finland and a war had started. The Germans helped the Finns and the Soviets were defeated, suffering a large number of casualties.

After I had been working at the resort a couple of months, a Jewish political officer spoke to me in Russian. I answered him in Ukrainian and he became very angry, calling me a word meaning Ukrainian, but in a derogatory way. He became so offensive that I got angry and called him a "bloody Jew". I didn't have anything against the Jews and only said that because I was angry with him. He said I had insulted his race and reported me straight away to the manager. The next day the police came to arrest me. They took me to Yalta in a police car and I was put in a cell for two days, then taken to court. After a very short hearing they sentenced me to one and a half years in a concentration camp.

* * *

I was taken to a big jail in Simferopol. After two weeks, the police collected 100 male prisoners and herded us into cattle trucks pulled by a special train. The train would stop from time to time to collect prisoners from other jails as it made its way very slowly across Ukraine and Russia, north to a town called Rybinsk. Inside the cattle trucks, they had rigged up shelves for the prisoners to sleep on. There were two at each side. There was no bedding of any kind and we had to put our fists under our heads for a pillow and sleep in whatever clothes we had. It was very cold and there was only one small stove, made from a bucket with holes in it. There were about forty people in each truck, so we huddled together to try to keep warm.

* * *

Our train arrived at the station, which was just outside the town. It was winter and very cold, with snow covering absolutely everything. We were told to get off the train and were marched in columns of about six men deep for about three kilometres to the concentration camp. There must have been about 2000 men altogether. The columns of prisoners marched to the square in the middle of the camp. I remember it was snowing. There was barbed wire surrounding the camp and towers with armed guards. Things had been arranged for us and some of the camp officials came outside with a list and split us into groups. I was with about fifty other people. We were assigned to a large barracks, which had the usual bunk beds on top of each other and were really only wooden shelves with no bedding. There were the same blood-sucking insects that lived at the camp near Archangel. When they jumped down and bit you, they left a big red mark and stank terribly when squashed.

We were given winter clothing when we arrived: a coat, trousers and a hat with material inside. The shoes were terrible. Some were made of string and others were made of old tyres. Mine were made of a sailcloth-like material and glued together. People sometimes tried to make shoes by putting as many cloths around their feet as they could; whatever type of shoe was worn, quite a lot of damage was done to people's feet and legs.

In the mornings we were woken at six o'clock. We went to breakfast and would each take a little bucket with us. We were given some very weak, slightly sweet tea, a piece of dry bread and, most of the time, some dried fish. We would go back to the barracks and eat it before assembling in the square at seven o'clock. The group leaders would check that everyone was there. If someone was sick, he would have to see a doctor who would only give time off if the person was very sick. It was almost impossible to get time off.

There were a lot of these camps all over the Soviet Union. The man who ran all the camps was a Jew called Rapaport, who was very well known as the big boss of the NKVD. Most of the prisoners were ordinary people, not criminals. The Soviet Government was the criminal, which used the people as slave labour.

Just after I arrived, a prisoner who had been there about eight years came to look at the new prisoners. He started talking to me and I found that he had lived in the next region in Ukraine to me. He told me I could join his group, which worked at a concrete factory looking after the conveyor belt. This was where they made the concrete used to build a dam for a hydroelectric station. There were about 200,000 people working around the area of the hydroelectric station and about 15,000 in our camp alone. I was very lucky because my work was indoors, which was much better than working outdoors in the snow. I was supposed to be working as a fitter, but I didn't know much about it so my friend said he would teach me. I would start the conveyor belt and see that materials, such as sand, arrived safely. Sometimes I had to go into the tunnel under the conveyor belt and open the door to let the sand go through the chute. If the conveyor was damaged, another man who also did this job and I had to repair the belt with clips. I also had to make sure that it was balanced properly and sometimes change the rollers.

The people who worked outside had to do very difficult work and many died. It was very cold and the ground was very hard.

Everything had to be done by hand, including the digging and the excavation, and anything that had to be moved — soil, sand, rocks or anything else — was moved by wheelbarrow. Some of these people came from Central Asia and a lot of them died. In Central Asia it is a lot warmer and these people were not used to bad weather and, of course, the very hard work. They had been fighting against the Soviet Government and were given twenty-five years in concentration camps when they were captured.

I was only a young boy, seventeen and a half years old, and I would have died if I'd had to work outside. My Ukrainian friend saved my life. His name was Gabriel Zaderko, a good yet ordinary country man who had been a store clerk on a collective farm. Two kilos of wheat couldn't be accounted for and although he had no idea why, he was blamed for the discrepancy and given ten years in this camp. He was no criminal; he had been a farmer before he had been forced onto a collective farm. He had a wife and four children, two boys and two girls, who he hadn't seen for eight years. He said I was about the same age as his eldest son and he was pleased to have been able to help me. He said I was as he imagined his son would be now.

Gabriel would tell me stories, saying that in New York and other large American cities, gangsters who robbed banks and committed other serious crimes rode about in beautiful cars and wore very fine clothes. I thought of criminals as being poor and shabby; I thought they lived like tramps. I found these stories hard to believe. He also told me about things he said would happen in the future. I respected his word but couldn't imagine some of the stories he told me. Once he told me that in the future there would be moving stairs and paths, to move from one place to another, and people wouldn't have to walk unless they wanted to. Of course, I thought he imagined these stories to make our difficult life a little easier. But I have lived long enough to see these things come about and when I stand on an escalator or travellator, I think of him. He also told me a time would come when people would be able to sit in a room, press a button and send rockets (which he described) to their intended target. He told me about something I didn't really understand at the time, but now that I have been remembering his words, I realise he was talking about lasers.

I've always been very grateful to this man and although there was no way I could repay him, I did my work as well as I possibly could so that everything ran smoothly. I worked there one and a half years and most of this time was the winter of 1940-1941. It was a terribly cold winter and bitterly cold working there. But at the end of February in the early spring, they let me go.

Paula, Andrii, Mama and Michael, 1936

*Andrii's mother,
Katerina, 1954*

*Andrii s father,
Jacob, 1952*

BOOK II

War

CHAPTER VIII

Reluctant soldier

I WAS given freedom papers, a small amount of money and a railway ticket to wherever I wanted to go. I decided to go home to my parents. I boarded the train to Ukraine but when it reached Moscow I decided to have a look around the city for a few days because I hadn't been there before. I went to see the very old Basilica, a church called St Basils in Red Square. I definitely did not go to Lenin's tomb, but I did see a large queue of people waiting to see it. I also went to the museum and the underground station called the Metro. It was very beautiful and clean and there were many marble statues and other works of art. It was very cheap — only twenty-five kopeks — and if you stayed underground and only travelled from station to station to look at the works of art and other things, you could stay all day for that price. There were also small kiosks where you could buy food and drink. I stayed in the Metro for about three hours, then boarded another train to Ukraine. I arrived at Melitopol, then caught a small bus for the last eighteen kilometres to my parents' new house. They were very pleased to see me back home. I had a bath and changed into better clothes and over supper, told them all that had happened to me.

Once I had settled in, I began work again on the collective farm with the rest of the family. I was there for about two and a half months when, in early May 1941, I received a letter telling me to report for a medical examination prior to my being called up into the services. Even if war had not been imminent, I would still have been called up to do military service as I was in my 19th year — I think that's why they let me out of the labour camp early. When I went for my medical examination, I was with five other boys my age. We had to strip naked and go into a room where there were four medical officers, two men and two women. Three of them just sat and looked at us and one of the women doctors checked every part of our bodies. Being young village boys, we found this extremely embarrassing. After the medical examination, we were told to go home.

The next day, a special messenger brought me a piece of paper which said I had passed the medical and had to report the next morning to the recruiting station — the same place where the medical had been carried out. This was May 7th, 1941. I was told to bring only toilet articles and shoe-cleaning implements. I arrived at the recruiting station about seven am and was shown to a room where I waited for half an hour with twenty other young men. We were all nineteen years of age and the military authorities had already decided, according to our education, height, health and other considerations, which branch of the services we would be assigned to. Someone gave us letters addressed to the units to which we were assigned. I was assigned to the army.

The collective farms in the area had provided five horse-drawn carts to take us to the railway station. I travelled in one cart with five others. We were given tickets and boarded the train. We were being taken to a town called Vynnytsia in Ukraine, a three-hour journey. The other young men I had seen boarded the same train, but were going to different destinations. I was with six other young men from my village. We knew each other and talked about our coming adventure in the army. We were all a bit nervous as we didn't know what was going to happen. When the train pulled into Vynnytsia station, an army sergeant was there to meet us. We walked with him to the army camp, which was only a kilometre away. He showed us where our barracks were and then we were taken to the quartermaster's store, where we were each given a uniform and an empty mattress. I was shown my bed — one of those double-decker ones — and given the top bunk.

The sergeant then took us to a field outside the barracks. He showed us a haystack and instructed us to half-fill our mattresses with straw. When we came back, he showed us how to put our uniforms on and how to sew a white piece of material onto the inside of our collars. We had to sew a fresh piece on every day. We were shown how to put on putties, which went around our ankles, and how to blacken them. They were like bandages and were the craziest pieces of clothing I had ever seen. I hated them. In the morning, when there was not much time, these putties were almost impossible to put on. We had to wind them over the top of our boots up to our knees. Some of the things that were said about these useless pieces of material cannot be printed. We found out later that the Germans had more modern gaiters, which were much easier to put on and were in a single piece with buckles.

Every morning at six o'clock the duty corporal shouted to get us up. We would put on our trousers, shoes and the terrible putties but no shirts. Then, no matter what the weather was like, we would go outside for fifteen minutes of exercises. After that we would wash ourselves in cold water, dry ourselves and finish dressing. We were not given much time to do this before we had to line up for inspection. After the inspection, if all was well, we could go to breakfast. We didn't get much breakfast and not much time to eat it either, never more than fifteen minutes. A usual breakfast would be bread and jam, tea and dried fish. Sometimes we would have boiled fish and occasionally porridge, semolina or fried sour cabbage. We went everywhere in columns of fifty men to breakfast, to exercises, to every meal. The only thing we could do by ourselves was go to the toilet or have a drink of water.

After breakfast we would go to a huge field for drill lessons — learning to march, when to stop, how to salute and how to turn. Every time we marched we had to sing until we were totally fed up with singing. Most of the songs we had to sing were Soviet political songs. If we didn't feel like singing or didn't sound good enough, some of the officers would make us march at double quick time as a punishment. If we had a good Ukrainian officer with us, we would be happy to sing Ukrainian songs and the singing would sound very good. One Ukrainian officer would let us sing Ukrainian songs as we marched and would take us to the river for a rest, where we would crack jokes and laugh and sing. We would have a couple of lookouts to make sure no Soviet political officer caught us.

* * *

One day in June 1941, an officer asked if anyone would like to learn to drive. I said I would, although I didn't know a thing about cars and had only been in one a couple of times. I was told to report to an area which was used as a driving school. I was only there for about two days, during which time they showed us the various parts of the cars and how to change tyres. We had no practice at all in actual driving. Someone put me into a lorry and told me to drive. Although I had told them I had a little driving skill, I really had no idea how to drive. When it was obvious I had no idea what I was doing, the officer swore at me, called me a liar and sent me back to my unit. I was very annoyed at the time, not getting the chance to learn to drive, but later on I was happy. Some of those men ended up driving the very heavy fuel tankers and, when the war started, the fuel tankers, which would drive in convoys, were a prime target for German aircraft, which blew most of them to smithereens.

* * *

I had been in the army for about two and a half months when, on July 22nd 1941 at ten am, Radio Moscow announced that the Germans had begun invading the Soviet Union and that Kiev, the capital of Ukraine, and quite a few other smaller towns in Ukraine, had been bombed. Consequently, the Soviet Union was at war with Germany. I didn't really know what war was like and I was worried and nervous, but not very frightened because I didn't really understand it or know what would happen.

We were issued with brand new semi-automatic rifles, still in their wooden boxes. The boxes were opened and we were handed the rifles covered in grease and told to clean them. We were then shown how to load and unload, disassemble and reassemble, and how to take care of them. We were given fifty rounds of ammunition which we wore on a belt around our waists, a small bayonet and two hand grenades resembling lemons, which were also worn on the belt. The hand grenades were the early type with separate fuses and had to be kept away from our ammunition. These fuses were like small pencils wrapped in cotton wool. We were told to put them in our shirt pockets and to be very careful as we could easily blow ourselves up. When these hand grenades were to be thrown, the fuses had to be inserted first, the pin pulled and the handle released before throwing them very quickly. These were not like the later ones which looked like baby pineapples and already had the fuses installed.

People were rushing around, panicking, and talking about war as they tried to prepare for it. Everything seemed to be disorganised. That evening we were given a lecture about war, which was mostly propaganda, by the political officer. At about five am the next day we were told to pack everything up and prepare for a long march. We were given dry emergency rations, a small flask of water and a small billy can each so we could cook our own meals. The blankets and mattresses were left behind but everything else was packed up and had to be carried with us. We were told to pack a couple of worn sheets in case we needed them for bandages. We also had to roll our overcoats up and slip them through a ring to carry them over our shoulders. We each had our rifle and all our ammunition, the hand grenades and the bayonets, as well as a heavy gas mask in a case and a small shovel. We were loaded down like horses.

The whole regiment lined up in columns and began the 200 kilometre march from Vynnytsia to Proskuriv, on the western border of Ukraine. It was the middle of summer and very hot, and as we marched along, we became very thirsty. But the people in charge of us wouldn't allow us to have much water claiming that the Germans may have poisoned it. This was stupid, the Germans hadn't even reached the area we were marching through, and even if there was a chance it was poisoned, there was much more risk that the men would die of thirst or heat exhaustion. We were exhausted and it was like marching through hell. Sometimes we were allowed to have some water but there was no way of testing it. We could only ask the villagers if the water was all right and if we could have some.

We marched for days and nights with very little rest. After a week we were completely worn out, and would be in no condition to fight when we arrived at Proskuriv. At night, we would march holding on to the next man, almost asleep on our feet and marching off the road and falling into gutters. Sometimes we were allowed only three hours sleep at a time. As we marched further the men began to throw things away, especially the heavy gas masks in cases. Over a period of time we threw nearly everything away, except our arms, ammunition and our really important overcoats which we used as our only bedding.

The wide main road was a never-ending parade of marching men, trucks and other military equipment which an army requires for war. Coming the other way were many refugee civilians, carrying and pushing many of their belongings on anything with wheels, herding their animals before them. It was a very sad sight to see. As we progressed further, each day we were allowed a little time to rest and eat. Sometimes the army kitchen would arrive with thick soup which had vegetables and a little meat. This was generally the only meal we would get for the day. If the horse-drawn kitchen got lost or didn't turn up we had to cook for ourselves using our emergency rations of dried soup cubes mixed with hot water. It was very odd that there were times when we were allowed water and at other times were forbidden it; in either case, we couldn't tell if the water was poisoned. Sometimes a car would drop off dry salted fish and dry biscuits. These were difficult to eat when we were not allowed to drink water. Another problem was that somebody had advised the authorities that drinking water would weaken us.

* * *

As we entered our second week on the road, it was still very hot and because most of the time we were not getting enough water, we were quite exhausted. We were told we were nearing the front line and we were ordered to stop and dig small holes, like foxholes, with just a little ground in front of our faces, and to prepare our grenades and other equipment. We could see a lot of smoke and burning on the fields in front of us. The Germans must have been a few kilometres away but we could hear a lot of noise from shooting and explosions. Behind us in proper trenches was the rest of the regiment. It was quite frightening and reminded me of the way you imagine a scene from hell or the end of the world. It almost seemed unreal.

We waited for about half an hour in our foxholes, then an order came from behind that we must prepare to withdraw. I put my equipment back on, strapped my overcoat across my back and started to run to the trenches behind me, bent double as we had been taught to do. When the Germans saw us withdrawing they advanced, bullets flying everywhere. I felt something slam into my right shoulder, like a red-hot iron, and jumped into the nearest trench. The men who were already there realised something had happened and removed my overcoat, rifle and took off my shirt. I had two wounds in my back — a small one where the bullet had entered and a larger one where it had exited. I was very lucky; if I had been running upright, the bullet would have gone right through my chest. The men thought two bullets had hit me and tried to stop the bleeding and patch my wound as best they could. A two-wheeled horse-drawn medical cart was not far away. There was no doctor but there was a medical assistant who seemed to know his job well. He bathed and disinfected my wounds and then bandaged all the way around my back, chest and over the shoulder, and put my arm in a sling.

We were near the River Horyn and could see a bridge, where a NKVD patrol waited to see no one deserted or crossed unless they were wounded. About two kilometres away, a hospital train waited to pick up injured soldiers from the area. I was allowed to cross with about six other men who were able to walk despite their wounds. We moved as quickly as we could and just managed to scramble on board the train, which left about half a minute after we climbed on. The train was so crowded we had to squeeze in.

The people in charge of the hospital train wanted to move out of the area as soon as possible because the front line was only a few kilometres away and the enemy was moving closer. We had gone about ten kilometres when we had to stop because the line had been blown up. A special unit of sappers was riding in the carriage just behind the engine and it took them three or four hours to repair the line.

The train was a passenger train with third-class carriages containing long wooden benches and corridors. There had been no changes made to make it into a hospital train, but it did have large Red Cross emblems on the roof and sides. The German pilots, whose aircraft were mostly Messerschmitt's, took no notice of the Red Cross emblems and sprayed the train with machine-gun fire. We were not going very fast and when the planes approached, the train would come to a dead stop. Those who could manage would get out and hide in the fields. I didn't bother to do this because there was just as much chance of getting hit doing that as staying on the train. Besides, I would have found it difficult to get on and off the train because I could only use one arm. My other shoulder and arm were very sore. The badly wounded people had to take their chances because they couldn't get off the train. Some people were killed and others were injured, but I was lucky and escaped further injury.

There were at least 200 wounded men on that train and only one doctor. There was virtually no medicine or anesthetic. In the four days between having my wounds dressed on the battlefield and finally arriving at the hospital, I didn't have my bandages changed or my wounds attended to, even though they had started to smell bad. Normally the journey would have taken only one day but, what with the bombing and strafing of the trains, chaos reigned for the entire journey and it took four times as long as it should.

Congestion on the rail lines was caused by troop trains going to the frontline and by trains taking Jewish refugees away from the danger area. These trains were given top priority and sometimes we were held up for hours. At one station one of the Jewish trains stopped alongside us. The windows on both trains were open and we noticed that a lot of the Jews were young men. I heard one of our company shout to them, 'Why aren't you going to the frontline to fight?' Someone from the other train shouted back, 'Our spirits are with the men who are fighting, but our bodies must take our families to safety.' Some of my companions asked the civilian refugees who stopped at our window if all the people had been evacuated. The refugees replied that all except those working on collective farms had been removed from danger. The officials considered the farm workers less than human and of no consequence, so they were left behind.

At the sides of the railway line were thousands of civilians, some panicking and all rushing away from the fighting with their belongings and herds of animals. Everywhere, especially at the stations, was in total chaos, while we could only sit in the train and watch. With so many trains, people and animals in the stations, the German fighter and light bomber pilots found very good opportunities to bomb and strafe such easy targets. At no time was there a Soviet aircraft in the sky to guard us.

An officer in the next carriage to us had been wounded by a hand grenade and had lost a considerable amount of flesh from his buttocks. He had lost a lot of blood and on the third day he started to smell very badly. There is no way to describe the smell of rotting flesh and gangrene unless you have experienced it. By now there was no medicine or anesthetic at all and although the officer was in one of the middle carriages, everyone on the train could smell it. Just before we arrived at Kiev he died. The train was stopped and he was buried in a very shallow grave at the side of the railway line. There was no religious service as there was no time, but I believe a few words were said. Even after he had been buried, the smell in the train lingered for days.

While we were travelling to Kiev we saw thousands more refugees on the road, some walking, some on horseback and others on tractors or horse-drawn carts; anything, in fact, they could use to get as far away as possible from the fighting. There were also lots of soldiers from disbanded units and herds of animals being moved, as well as farm animals roaming around by themselves. The refugees were victims of Stalin's scorched earth policy, which meant anything that might be of use to the Germans had to be destroyed. The NKVD was in charge of this policy and all fields, wheat silos, grain stores, warehouses, ordinary houses and any farm buildings were burnt to the ground. The tractors, cars, harvesters and other farm equipment was blown up with hand grenades. Railways which were not being used were destroyed too. The last train to leave the frontline had a huge hook attached to it and to the wooden sleepers so that they would all be torn up and destroyed as the train left. The NKVD also burnt all the jails housing political prisoners with the prisoners still trapped inside. In Karkov, 1200 people were burnt to death, while in Vynnytsia 400 people met their death in the same way. I was told about these atrocities by many different people and later I read the same stories in newspapers and books.

* * *

When we arrived at Kiev railway station, many civilians rushed up to the hospital train. The war had only been raging for a few weeks and this was the very first train to arrive with wounded soldiers. People gathered around to see if anyone they knew was on board. They all asked us for news of what was happening and if we had seen any of their relatives. They gave us gifts of sweetbread rings and rolls, soft drinks, biscuits, cigarettes, tobacco, matches and lots of flowers, as well as packets of writing paper and envelopes and hand-embroidered hankies. A person's own hand embroidery is always an honoured gift in Ukraine. Many civilians were crying and we were very grateful for their gifts and were touched by their feelings and generosity.

The train stood in Kiev station for about an hour before we set off again and the civilian crowd had to disperse. Almost everyone on board needed hospital treatment and our journey had already been too long. We travelled for about four hours and arrived at a small town called Myrhorod, which means "peace town". There was a small hospital and about half the wounded, including myself, were taken there while the rest went somewhere else. I was taken with the other wounded men to a room where the doctors, sisters and nurses were waiting for us. Some people were left in the corridor on stretchers while the medical staff arranged where everyone was to go. The doctors came round and checked everyone to see what needed to be done and the most severely wounded were prepared for the operating theatres.

When it was my turn, a sister took my shirt off then started to remove my bandages, but they were stuck to my skin and smelt very nasty. She asked me how long they had been on and when I told her four days, she moistened the old bandages, trying to gently pull them off. It was quite a painful procedure and resulted in both wounds bleeding again. She bathed them and applied clean bandages. She put my arm in a sling again and told me to move it as little as possible. Two other nurses washed me in a bath, being careful to keep my bandages dry, then helped me into a pair of pyjamas. My clothes had been so dirty they were put in a sack and thrown away. One of the nurses showed me to a ward with six beds. This ward was for people with minor injuries and five of the beds were already occupied. She helped me into bed and I had to lie on my stomach or on my left side. About half an hour later they brought us a very nice hot meal and while I can't remember what food we ate, I do remember having difficulty eating the food with my left hand. We all enjoyed the food because it was quite a long time since we had eaten a real meal.

* * *

I stayed in the hospital for two weeks and then those with minor wounds were taken by train to Donbas, a very large coal mining area with many towns. We went to a hospital in a town called Artemivsk. The hospital was five storys high and had very large wards. By this time I had started to move out of bed as much as possible and would go to the canteen for meals. I was able to visit the library which was also a games room where you could play cards, dominoes, chess, drafts and other games. There was also a piano. Most of the Ukrainians would gather around and sing old Ukrainian songs slowly and quietly at first. Then we would end up singing very loudly. Sometimes the Soviet political officer would hear and order us to stop. If the Russians sang Soviet political songs, that was allowed and encouraged.

X-rays were taken to see if any bones or muscles had been damaged in my shoulder or back. Fortunately there was no major damage and the wounds started to heal normally. However, because my arm had been immobilised for so long, I was unable to move it. A sister massaged it and moved it about, helping me to exercise by doing all sorts of things that would now be called physiotherapy. It was terribly difficult to do and very painful and sometimes I nearly cried. The sister encouraged me and insisted that the exercising was to be done every day for half an hour for about three weeks. 'If you don't do the exercises you will never be able to move your right arm again,' she said. She may have told me this to frighten me into trying harder.

Most of the soldiers were older than me, although there were a few my age, and many of us were from different units. It was very interesting to listen to the stories of the soldiers' lives, their adventures and the battles they had fought. I stayed at the hospital about six weeks and by that time, my back was healing well and my shoulder and arm were working properly. I was then discharged from hospital and taken with other men to an army camp where new units were being formed. Before we left the hospital we were issued with whatever they could find for us to wear; a motley assortment of civilian clothes, uniforms and shoes, most likely scavenged from the bodies of dead people.

CHAPTER IX

Stalin's slave

WE travelled by train for about an hour and a half. Our destination was Mariupol, where I had worked during my earlier years. After disembarking from the train we marched about two kilometres to a large park on the outskirts of the town where about fifty large tents had been pitched.

The army authorities had already started to form new units. A few soldiers had been tank crews and were formed into a tank unit, and one or two pilots were taken away to join air crews. But most of us were infantry men, sent there from hospitals and disbanded units, so we were all formed into new units. I stayed there one week while we were being issued with uniforms, rifles and ammunition. We were given odd jobs, such as helping to peel potatoes in the kitchen. We also had to exercise and go to political lectures. Because there was a good field kitchen we ate very well. When we had some spare time we would read newspapers, listen to the radio and go for walks in the town. The town was preparing for an attack — the Germans were not far away. Mariupol is a large town and had many factories and the machinery was being moved out and taken away by train. The civilians were digging long wide anti-tank traps around the town. Everyone was rushing around because they knew the frontline was swiftly getting closer.

One day I was walking with four other young men on the outskirts of the town when we came upon a large tomato field belonging to a collective farm. We saw twelve young girls picking the tomatoes so we started to laugh, joke and tease them

— anything to relieve the tension. They seemed to enjoy the banter and after joking with us started to throw tomatoes at us. They asked us to help them pick the fruit but we were due back at our base.

Some of us who had already been at the frontline would show off to the young new recruits, saying we had experienced the smell of gunpowder, even though most of us hadn't done any real fighting. I didn't want to go back to the frontline. I was a little frightened, but the real reason was that I hated the idea of fighting for Stalin and the communists who had broken up my family and my country. We Ukrainians were not allowed to have our own identity and were even discouraged from using our own language. I didn't feel I was fighting for my country — we were slaves to another country.

Some of our units were left to defend the town, but I was among those who had to move out. We joined the main battalion of about 1000 men in Marioupol and then we all travelled by train across Ukraine and north to the Bransk district of Russia. Once when our train had stopped at a station, German planes started to strafe us. A train next to us carrying a large container full of methylated spirits, was peppered full of holes and the methylated spirits started to leak. Our soldiers drank some of it and filled their flasks with it, and some of us drank from our helmets. I thought I would try it so I diluted it fifty-fifty with water. I drank a little but it tasted horrible so I decided not to have any more. It made us all very drunk and we were all singing and making a lot of noise. Some of the men vomited. Our train then started moving. Men who had drunk the methylated spirits full strength died in great pain about four hours later. We didn't know it then but methylated spirits burns a person's insides. The bodies were taken off the train and our officer told us off, making us throw it all away. I had already decided not to drink any more but the next day, every time I drank water, I felt drunk again because there was still too much spirit in my body. This must have been early autumn 1941.

After two days we arrived at a small town called Karachev, near Bransk. We left the train and were loaded into open-back lorries, covering ourselves with branches and leaves as camouflage. I didn't think this provided much camouflage as any plane could have easily seen the moving lorries. Our destination was a forest, where we covered the lorries with branches and erected small tents. The mobile field kitchen was with us and we had a hot meal, after which we checked our rifles and ammunition and prepared everything in case of attack. We had some spare time, so some of the younger men and I climbed the tall, slender birch trees, bending them with our weight until we were on the ground, then hopping off quickly and watching as they slowly sprang back. This was rather childish but it was the sort of thing we had done as children and we were not very old.

We stayed there half a day, then formed into columns and marched a couple of kilometres to a small village. The frontline was not very far away and just outside the village we started to dig trenches and make other preparations for a defence line. Our officer told us to sit and wait in the trenches because the Germans were moving toward us. From where we were sitting, we could look down on a small village. Between us and the village was a tiny stream with a small bridge and a water mill with a large wheel.

The next day our officer ordered me and two others to go to the village and ask for food, so we crossed the bridge to the village. We were directed to a small bakery not very far away and the baker told us to come back in the afternoon, by which time he would have baked some bread for us. We went back to our trenches and waited until after midday then went back to the bakery. The baker had made six large flat loaves and because we were soldiers, we were given them for free. We put the bread in a couple of sacks and were about to go back to the trenches when one of the village women told us there was traffic coming which could be Germans. She suggested that we hide behind her house. We had approached the villagers unarmed and there were only the three of us so we did as she suggested.

As we looked out at the road from behind the house, we saw advance scouts of the German army coming down the road. There were two motorbikes and two cars with officers standing up in them, looking through binoculars. They didn't see us or the trenches full of our fellow soldiers in the background. The Germans looked around the village but they didn't bother to get down from their vehicles. They then turned around and drove back the way they had come. When they had gone, we picked up the bread and returned to our trenches.

We told our officer about the Germans, but he and all the men had already seen them. We cut up the bread and shared it around in our own section. The other soldiers in our battalion were spread around in other trenches further away. As we sat quietly eating the bread, we saw a large heavily-armoured column of Germans on the road. There were motorbikes, armoured cars and half a dozen tanks, but mostly lorries full of soldiers. We only had rifles, so our officers and NCOs told us not to shoot. We just sat there and watched them go by. We had no field telephone or radio or any other form of communication with anyone outside our area.

Our Ukrainian lieutenant — we didn't know our officers' names, we were only allowed to call officers by their ranks — had been a teacher and part-time soldier when he was called up. He was made a lieutenant because he was very intelligent. I don't know how he found out — maybe from the scouts — but about half an hour after we had seen the Germans go past, he told us we were now far behind the German lines. We were cut off and surrounded by the enemy because the Germans had advanced at an incredible speed. Some of our NCOs wanted us to make a charge and try to break out, but the Ukrainian lieutenant said we would all be killed. The Germans were heavily armed with machine guns and all sorts of heavy armory including anti-aircraft guns, whereas we only had rifles. The lieutenant told us that our best chance was to break up — it was every man for himself. He told us it was better than being taken prisoner or getting killed in a charge, and said that we could do what we liked. He suggested we try to go home or join the partisans, if we could find them.

* * *

Four young men and I walked south towards Ukraine. At the first village we came to, we gave our rifles and ammunition to an old man and asked for food in exchange. He told us to go to the collective farm, where we asked at the office for some food. They looked in the storeroom and gave us about three kilograms of uncooked meat, two dozen eggs and a loaf of bread. We asked a woman at a nearby house if she would cook the food for us. She took the food, threw the meat in some water and cracked all the eggs in it as well. It cooked for an hour while we sat smoking outside, then she called us in and plonked the food on the table. It was awful. The meat was in one piece and wasn't properly cooked and the eggs were all through the water. It was impossible to eat it and we were very angry about the waste. We said a couple of rude words to this Russian woman, who we thought had spoilt the food deliberately. 'Are you going to waste food?' she asked us, but except for the bread it was impossible to eat it.

We left, and soon after spied a stray piglet, which was about a year old. We drove it before us with a small stick and when we reached the end of the village asked a man in the last house if he would swap the piglet for some food. He gave us a piece of cooked fat bacon, some bread, a lump of honeycomb in wax paper and two packets of tobacco. We were happy with this and he was happy to have the pig. The five of us sat in a field and ate this meal. We talked while we ate and decided to split up, three of my companions deciding to travel together to their own villages.

The other soldier was a young Russian called Ivan who was about my age. He told me his family lived in Stepanivka, the village where I was born. It was further south than Terpania, where my family now lived and where I was headed. I didn't know him but as we were going in the same direction we decided to travel together. The Soviets had always tried to place as many Russian families in Ukraine as possible, but this was no fault of Ivan's. Apart from the fact that the five of us needed to go in different directions, it was better for small groups of two or three to move together as it was easier to hide. It was also easier for people to feed us and for us to live off the land. Ivan and I said goodbye and good luck to the other three and started on our long walk home.

We had no choice but to walk even though we knew how dangerous it was behind enemy lines. We might have been shot as partisans even though we had no weapons, or as spies even though we were in uniform. Anything can happen in war time. We had to take the risk — what would be would be — and we just walked and hoped for the best. We were not frightened of wolves or other animals, as there were no dangerous ones in the area. Anyhow, as I said to Ivan, 'Humans are the most dangerous animals.'

After a few days we came to a small forest and found a little hut. There was nothing inside except a large school-type map on the floor. I tore a piece off which had Ukrainian territory on it. (I've always been fascinated by maps and I like geography. I would have liked to have been a map maker or some sort of surveyor if I'd had an education.) Just outside the forest was another small village. We approached a house where two men told us they were trying to form a partisan group and asked us to join them. We knew immediately they were Soviet officers. They wore no officers' insignia but their expensive leather coats and the weapons they were carrying gave them away. They left us, saying they had business to attend to, but asked that we wait at the house for them to come back. As soon as they left, the people who owned the house gave us food and drink and told us the officers were communists — most of the village folk, including those present, hated them.

We left as soon as we had eaten. It was late evening and was becoming quite dark. Autumn had set in — it must have been early November 1941. We couldn't stay in the village because of the communist partisans and it was difficult to cross the forest in the dark. We saw a small haystack that the village people had stacked to dry for the animals to eat, so we made two holes in the side of the hay and went to sleep. It was warm and we slept well, but when we emerged from the haystack the next morning, everything was covered in snow. We didn't follow the road but travelled across the forest and fields for about two days before coming to a village between two belts of forest. We called at a house and were allowed to sleep in the shed and we were given food. There were a lot of forests in this area, with quite a few large cleared fields in between.

We left that village and two days later came upon what must have been a recent battleground. There were bodies everywhere and quite a few dead horses still harnessed to their carts. There were about a dozen harnessed horses still alive. Some others had saddles and were standing around in the field. We freed all the horses, took their saddles off and let them go. We were sure that the village people would find them. We thought of taking two horses, or a horse and cart, but decided it was much easier to hide on foot. Even if we rode horses over the countryside, we would still be conspicuous. We didn't take anything from the dead and left there as quickly as possible.

* * *

Of course, we had to be very careful as we were still behind enemy lines. And one day, as we were walking on a small country road, six soldiers, aboard a small German lorry with a canvas top, came towards us. They were checking communication links and telephone wires. There was no time to hide, so we didn't try to run away in case they shot us. The lorry stopped and one of the soldiers decided he wanted our boots. They were knee-high boots and had been given to us with our uniforms, so they were still quite new. There was nothing I could do when the soldier told me to take them off. He tried them on but they were too big, so he gave them back. Then he tried on Ivan's boots, which fitted him perfectly. He gave Ivan some very poor quality shoes in exchange. The other Germans didn't ask to try on my boots. None of us understood each other very well, but the Germans made us understand there was a small camp nearby. They must have thought we wanted to surrender, so we let them think that was where we were going. As soon as the lorry was out of sight, we hurried in the opposite direction to the one they had told us to go.

Not far away there was a dam which had been bombed. The water had flooded the fields to a depth of about fifteen centimetres, or six inches. We had to cross the fields and I was lucky my boots hadn't been taken by the Germans. It was impossible for Ivan to cross without getting soaked, so I carried him on my back for about 300 metres until we reached higher ground where there was no water. From there we saw a village on the border of Russia and Ukraine. At last we had reached Ukrainian territory. There was a small river, which we had to cross to reach the village, so we walked down the bank and saw an old man who had a rowing boat which he used to carry people to the other side. There were already some people on board. We also noticed that the boat owner was quite drunk. He asked for money, but I only had half of what he wanted so I told Ivan to get in the boat and paid the old man Ivan's fare. I started to push the boat away and at the last minute jumped on board. The old man gave me a dirty look, but I took the oars and did the rowing for him in lieu of money.

When we reached the other side I knew immediately we really were in Ukraine. The houses were made of the same mud brick as the one my family had built on the collective farm. I started talking to an elderly couple, who asked me where I came from. They didn't come from the same place as me but, like me, they were from the south of Ukraine. They had owned a farm and had also been considered *kulaks*. They had settled in this small village on the border after travelling around a bit. They asked us into their house and gave us some warm, milky, sweet pudding and bread. It was very tasty and we enjoyed it.

These two people were very pleasant and very generous. They didn't have very much food themselves, yet managed to find us a piece of bacon, some bread, dried fruit and a little tobacco which they put into linen bags. They told us we should be wearing civilian clothes and the husband gave us some of his own clothes. He did not have enough for both of us so he went to the house next door where the people gave him some more. He managed to get us shirts, jackets, trousers and caps, but we didn't throw our uniforms away. We wore the civilian clothes on top because we knew we would encounter very cold weather on our journey. The elderly couple and the middle-aged couple from next door gave us directions and came outside to see us off, wishing us all the very best on our journey.

* * *

We started walking again and consulting the map, kept moving south. We came to a small town called Sumy a few days later. There were a few Germans there, but nobody took any notice of us. We then decided that travelling through the countryside would be safer and there was more chance of being given food. We walked and walked, across villages and down country roads and managed to get enough food along the way. We just kept moving and the weather kept getting colder. Even though Ivan had such terrible footwear, neither of us had trouble with our feet, but we were very dirty. It was too cold to wash in the rivers and the streams so we became infested with lice. Most people therefore, made us sleep in the stables or outhouses, which just made the problem worse.

After a couple more weeks walking, we came to another small town called Krasnograd, which was on both sides of a large river. This river originally had four bridges, but three of them had been blown up. The fourth was intact, but had six Germans guarding it — two at the entrance, two in the middle and two at the end. We had to get across somehow, but we knew we would never get past the soldiers. We had no papers of any sort and were without any type of pass. We thought of stealing a boat, but that was very dangerous. We would probably have been shot on sight. So stealing a boat was out, the other bridges were down and the river was too wide and cold to swim across. Of course, we would have been in everybody's sight if we had tried to swim. We were edging closer when a middle-aged woman walked in front of us with two full buckets of water. This is considered a very good omen and she said we would have good luck on our journey home. I believed her and I think Ivan did, too. We thanked her for her good wishes.

We decided to brazen it out and walked at a normal pace towards the bridge. The first two Germans ignored us. When we came to the middle two guards, they also took no notice. The last two Germans also ignored us, and we were across! It was very hard to believe we had not been challenged, almost as if we were invisible. Ivan and I both believed, and I still believe, this happened because of our good luck charm, who carried two buckets of water across our path. Hidden by high hedges, we ran as quickly as we could to put the bridge far behind us. We went through the town and kept going for about six kilometres. Evening was falling as we entered a small village, hoping to find food and shelter. Almost immediately we were arrested by the local police who asked for our documents, but we had thrown them away, thinking they might cause us problems. We told the police our story, but they said they must lock us up until the morning.

A police guard was put on the door. Inside there were six other prisoners, all middle-aged men. There was a lot of forest in the area where the partisans hid, and the prisoners told us the police must have thought we were scouts for them. They also said that power had gone to the head of the German commandant. His word was law and he did just what he liked. The people of the village were scared of him. The prisoners were all local people who were accused of only small crimes. One had killed a pig without giving the authorities the skin, but nobody seemed to know why the Germans wanted a pigskin. It was really quite ridiculous. Others had pretended to be sick to avoid work on the collective farm and had been found out. The Germans had kept the collective farms, they told us, and were treating the people in the same way as the Soviets.

The room we were in was not a real cell, and the other prisoners suggested we escape, as we would probably be sent to a prison or concentration camp. Ivan and I asked if any of them wanted to come with us, but they refused because they were middle-aged men and didn't want to move away from their homes. They had only been accused of minor crimes, so they didn't expect to be shot or receive harsh punishment. They knew the Germans needed them to work on the collective farm. So in the middle of the night when the duty policeman had fallen asleep, Ivan and I managed to pry open the window with Ivan's small knife and squeeze through. The weather was very bad, windy and raining. It was very dark but we knew which way we had to go and kept to the road, trying to get as far away as possible from that village.

* * *

We walked about fifteen kilometres before morning started to break. It was still windy and drizzling slightly. By the time we reached a rather large village it was about ten am. We could see smoke coming from the cottage chimneys. At one of the first cottages we asked for food and the people asked us to sit at the table while they gave us freshly-baked bread, cheese and milk. When we were ready to go they gave us dried fruit and bread, a piece of salted dried meat and some tobacco. We used any sort of paper, even newspaper, to roll the tobacco to make our cigarettes. And being smokers we always had matches with us. We didn't stop to rest, even though we'd had no sleep at all — we just wanted to leave this area behind us as soon as we could. We walked south for about twenty kilometres, passing through two villages that day, and by the time we reached the third village it was growing dark. It was late autumn and growing dark quite early, so we started to look for somewhere to sleep because it was too cold to sleep outside.

We came to a nice-looking house, knocked on the door and asked the lady if there was anywhere we could sleep. We expected her to show us to a stable or shed, but she asked us inside. She gave us some bread and very nice borsch, which had been left over from the day before. She also gave us some milk pudding, but we could hardly eat it, we were so tired we kept falling asleep at the table. She showed us to a spare room with a single bed made up with home-made blankets. She then went next door and came back with her friend. Both women were in their early 30s and very attractive. Their husbands were away, probably fighting in the war. They started undressing and made it quite obvious that they would have liked to sleep with us. However, we were very tired indeed and also shy because we were full of lice. The women made a makeshift bed for themselves in the same room as us, with Ivan and myself on the single bed. We were absolutely dead tired and slept like logs.

When we awoke it was quite late in the morning and the women had made breakfast. They asked us to stay a few days but although we would have liked to, we decided we should move along. We wanted to get home and we didn't know how danger-ous it would be to stay in one place for too long. We also wanted to cover as much distance as possible before winter set in. We said goodbye and thanked them very much for the food and the bed. As we walked along we talked about how we would have liked to stay a few more days. We may have even been able to have a bath! In those days, especially in the country areas, it took quite a while to prepare a bath and if we had stayed we would have enjoyed the opportunity to have a bath each. We confided in each other that we wouldn't have minded taking the young ladies up on their other offer, but I think we were just talking "boy's talk".

* * *

We decided not to cross any more towns. It was too dangerous and people in towns and cities didn't have much food, whereas the country people could always find something for us. So we just walked and walked and walked, crossing lots of small villages, and almost everyone we asked managed to give us some food, no matter how little they had. The Ukrainian people are very generous and they were happy to help two soldiers who had been at the front and who were trying to make their way home.

The countryside was very beautiful, although the weather was getting colder, and we were drawing very close to the village of Terpenia, where my parents now lived. We arrived at a small railway crossing about seven kilometres from the village and saw three men on a small horse-drawn cart. We asked if they were going near Terpenia. They were, and they offered us a lift which we refused as we wanted to enter the village in darkness. However, they had a pencil and paper and agreed to deliver a note to my family, explaining where I was and asking that baths be prepared for my friend and I.

Sometime later, as we drew closer to the village, we saw a large horse-drawn cart with lots of people on board coming home from work. I thought I saw my father among the crowd on the back of the cart, but he didn't recognise me. The driver asked us if we wanted a lift, but we told him we did not have far to go and that there were too many people on the cart already. We didn't tell him we didn't want to get on in case we gave the people lice.

CHAPTER X

Homecoming

FROM the time our unit was disbanded until the time we
reached my village, Ivan and I had walked approximately
1800 kilometres — 150 kilometres from Russia to the Ukrainian border and then almost all the way across Ukraine. We
walked the whole way and it took us just over six weeks. Although
it was autumn, the weather had been reasonable because we
were travelling south all the time. We had heard a lot about the
scorched earth policy while on the road, but we only saw exam-
ples of it in the north. Some of the beautiful and famous pine
forests had been torched, but in most of the areas we travelled,
the victorious Germans had moved with such incredible speed
that the Soviets had not had time to carry out their orders. And,
as we continued south, we found that the people had ignored
instructions when the NKVD were not around to supervise them.

When we finally entered Terpenia we found a crowd of people
waiting to greet us; Mama, Tato, my sister Frossia, my girlfriend
Olga, our next-door neighbours and people from over the road,
as well as a few other friends and neighbours. Ivan was to set off
again for his village in the morning and, even though Ukraine —
including our village — was occupied by Germans, I thought I
might be able to mix unnoticed with the other villagers. However
Frossia, in her excitement, had told quite a lot of people.

We went inside the house to eat and have a bath. After a wash
we sat down to borsch and milk pudding. While we ate, water
for a bath was heating on the stove. Only one person could have

a bath at a time, so we offered to let Ivan bath first but he said he was too tired. He may also have been shy as there was not much room in the house. The bath was a long wooden trough, used for bathing and also for washing clothes. My clothes were rolled up and put outside and some old clean clothes were brought for me. I was very tired, so Mama helped me bathe. When she saw the wounds on my back, she cried. They were only partly-healed and she thought they looked inflamed. I told her not to worry; it was only three months since I was wounded and I was healing well. In that time they had given me only slight pain on our long walk home and were getting better every day.

Since it was very dark, we gave Ivan some clean clothes and made a bed up for him in the corridor because there was very little room in the house and he didn't want to leave lice. Ivan was looking forward to getting home. He had told me that he and his wife were expecting their first child and that he should have a new baby by now. He had only forty kilometres to travel and he thought it would take him two days, so he wanted to start out as early as possible the next day. The next day, after breakfast, he was ready to leave. We wished him good luck and gave him some food and a bottle of water to take with him.

* * *

I was glad to find that the small village of Terpenea hadn't suffered any damage at all. The fighting had passed it by, it was very out of the way, like Stepenevka. The church in Terpenea was still intact but had been used as a dance hall and club — by the time I had walked home the villagers had restored it as a church and had it rededicated. It was quite a small church, but large enough for the small village. My family and I went there the next day to give thanks for my safe return. In the 1930s, the communists destroyed many Ukrainian churches all over the country, including the very beautiful and ancient churches in the cities. Some of the very large cathedrals were stripped of anything considered to be religious before being turned into museums. The same happened in the country areas. The church in my maternal grandparents' village was razed to the ground and the one in Stepanevka was used as a grain store. As soon as the people had a chance to do so, they restored the churches and the clergy re-consecrated them.

My family brought me up to date on the village news. The German commandant had taken up residence in the council offices. He was armed at all times and had no German staff, just a staff of Ukrainian villagers who were forced to work for him. One man had been chosen as his interpreter because he spoke passable German. The commandant and translator would come to the collective farms to issue the German authorities orders. They didn't interfere in the villagers' lives to a great extent as long as all orders were obeyed and everyone did their work properly. I started work at the collective farm, the same one I had worked on before I was called up. Tato and Frossia also worked there and my mother took care of the home duties. Michael was still away at trade school in Zaporizhya.

I had been home a week when a man who had been travelling in the huge coal mining area of Donbas returned home to the village. Everyone was talking about the things he said. The Germans had advanced swiftly in the Donbas area and 300 students from a trade school in Zaporizhya were evacuated under the supervision of the NKVD. However, the Germans moved into a circle and blocked the roads, cutting off the students' retreat. The NKVD forced the students into a small valley and mowed them down with machine-gun fire, not wanting their knowledge to fall into the hands of the Germans. The NKVD men then disappeared — rumour had it they had an aeroplane waiting.

After the massacre the local people gave the students a proper burial. They also found a few of the boys badly wounded but still alive. They cared for the boys, tending their wounds and hiding them from the Germans, or in case the NKVD murderers came back. In later years, communist broadcasts and newspapers blamed the Germans for this and other massacres. We had not heard from Michael and feared that he was one of those killed. We were upset and worried, but we still hoped. You can never be sure of anything in war.

Before I was called up to join the army I had been very friendly with a girl called Olga who lived across the road. We decided to become "steady" friends, but she was quite young and we had not become lovers. After I had been home for a short while, my sister and some friends told me that when a Red Army unit had been stationed in our village, Olga had taken more than a passing interest in quite a few of the men and had earned herself a very bad name with the villagers. I asked mother if this was true — I knew she would not tell a lie. She confirmed this story and suggested I drop Olga, who seemed to have acted in a very bad way. The whole family suggested I didn't see her as a girlfriend. I thought about it and decided they were right. She came over to our house a few times, pretending to be visiting Frossia. After a while she realised that I wasn't interested in her anymore and stopped coming.

There were no dividing fences on the collective farm. One afternoon, when Tato was on another job, the supervisor told me the horses were in the wheat and to get them out. There was an old horse called Cantar who was a real troublemaker, and I suspected he had led the other horses to where they knew they shouldn't be. I rode a fine young chestnut colt around the outside of the field and shouted to the loose horses. They all wandered over to their stables, except that old devil Cantar. He headed towards where I was sitting astride my horse and before I realised what he was doing he kicked my horse in the chest, then kicked me on the left calf. He then put his tail up and galloped for the stables. I thought my leg was broken, and slowly rode over to the stables, not knowing how badly my horse was injured. I tried to dismount, but I couldn't put my left leg on the ground and had to hop. Surprisingly, my horse had only a slight cut and seemed to be all right. I was so angry that I tied Cantar up and gave him some hard slaps with my hand. I was hopping about all the time and left him tied up, which I knew he didn't like. Thankfully my leg wasn't broken but it was very swollen for more than a week and very badly bruised. I could walk very slowly, but with a great deal of pain. I still have dark blue marks on my leg after all these years.

* * *

It was now the winter of 1941-1942 and there was still a lot of work that we could do outside on the farm, even though snow had started to fall. Mostly we brought in the products from the fields and packed them into huge storage sheds. We had to work hard to save everything before the whole landscape was completely covered in snow. We villagers were allowed to have a few vegetables, such as potatoes and beetroot, and also the dried husks and other offcuts of sweet corn and sunflowers for our fires. As winter progressed we started working indoors, repairing the houses and storerooms, general storage jobs and cleaning up. In the past, during the very deep winter, we played indoor games, told jokes and stories, sang and played musical instruments and sat around eating sunflower kernels. Weather permitting, we would go visiting and sometimes the whole community would put on a play in one of the larger houses.

Christmas Day came around on January 7th 1942, followed by

New Year on January 14th. The Ukrainian Orthodox Church still follows the old calendar for its church celebrations and the Germans had not forbidden any religious observations. In the past, the communists had forbidden us to celebrate religious festivals, but many people, especially the older folks, had quietly done so for years. We tried to make it as good a Christmas as we could. Tato and I began making homemade whisky about two weeks before Christmas, even though this was an illegal act. Before collectivisation, the women folk would spend weeks preparing food and we would visit other houses in the village, carol singing and chanting blessings. This year, Mama and Frossia prepared the food the day before Christmas and most people stayed in their own homes. No one felt like celebrating because we were under occupation and many men from the village were missing.

When spring began we gave all the fruit trees a light pruning and placed straw at intervals between the trees, covering it with soil. When the straw was lit the dense smoke protected the new blossoms from early morning frost — there was an old belief that smoke was good for trees, helping fruitfulness. Some elderly men had the job of keeping an eye on the weather. Every morning at four am they would check for frost and if there was any, they would light the straw. There was very little flame because of the soil on top.

There was plenty of work to be done in the orchards. More pruning and picking up branches, weeding and turning the soil over around the trees. It was still too early for sowing seeds; we couldn't work in the fields until about the end of March when the ground had dried out. Tato still had the job of caring for the horses, and although we had plenty of work to do we did have some spare time.

The German authorities had given their permission for a dance to be held in one of the larger houses. Many young people attended and although I couldn't dance, I decided to take my sister, Frossia. It was very lively and great fun. The young folk danced, sang, ate, drank and told jokes. Although I didn't dance I enjoyed the lively atmosphere. I started talking to a young widow called Olga. She was nineteen and I was nineteen and a half and we talked for quite a long time. She said she was hot so we walked in the cool, fresh air for a while. It started to get chilly and rain began to drizzle, so we sheltered in a hay shed. We sat down on the fresh straw together and she called me pet names, teasing me for being shy. We kissed and after a while we made love. It may seem a strange thing for a man to say, especially as she was younger than me, but I felt as if she had taken advantage of me. I wasn't really complaining, but I felt uneasy. She wasn't a girl I would have chosen to be with; in fact I didn't really like her, even though she was young and pretty.

* * *

The whole of Ukraine was under German control since the communists had retreated to Russia, so in May 1942 my family tried to get our old house in Stepanivka back, which had been taken from us when we were sent to the labour camp. We thought the Ukrainian council leaders in Stepanivka might be able to help us. We explained to the collective farm authorities what we wanted to do and Tato and I managed to get five days off. We decided to walk the forty kilometres to Stepanivka because the weather was good and we couldn't borrow any of the farm horses at such a busy time. The journey would take us two days each way and we would stay overnight on the way there and back at a small village with a family who had been friends to us for many years; they had even known Tato before he was married. That left us one day for business and for visiting friends and family.

When we arrived in Stepanivka, we dropped in to see my sister, Tatyana, and her family. She knew her husband Gregory used to beat me but guessed that I hadn't told the rest of the family. We also visited Ivan, whom I had walked home with, and his wife and they proudly showed us their new son. We stopped to have a look at our old house. Because the village was by the seaside, our house had been used as a fishing collective. Two walls had been knocked down and there was evidence of boats and nets that had been repaired there. It was no longer a fishing collective, but now a fisherman and his family were living there.

We then met with the Ukrainian village councillors, telling them our story and asked for the return of our house. The councillors were friends from years ago and had also been thrown off their farms, so we had no trouble convincing them to allow us to have our old home. In fact, they seemed very pleased to do this for us. We were given some official papers and went straight back to the house to show them to the fisherman. He was not happy, but said if they had to move they would and would let the council know when they had done so. We reported this back to the councillors, who said they would send a message as soon as the house was vacated. We walked back to Terpenia, arriving home quite late in the evening, five days after setting out. We felt we had done quite well and we were all pleased that we had encountered no problems.

Although we could have the house back, the land and all the animals and equipment belonged to a collective farm, now owned by the Germans. However, no German officials or military personnel lived in Stepanivka. There was one German man, who we were told to call the commandant, who often came to issue orders to the collective farm supervisor and council officials. He must have been in his fifties and although he was always in uniform, we guessed he had been a farmer before the war because he knew about farming, which was more than could be said for our previous communist bosses.

The house in Terpenia belonged to us. We had been given the land before the war and had built the house ourselves, so we sold it once we received word that our Stepanivka house was vacant. The letter from the council said the fisherman's family had found a house in another village, but they were not happy about moving because they had been living in our house rent-free. We got a fairly good price for the Terpenia house and rented a cart drawn by two horses to move our belongings to Stepanivka. There were a lot of repairs that needed to be done at the house, starting with the two walls that had been knocked down. We made one of these into a double wall, so that parts of the stove could fit inside and warm both rooms as it had done before. Some of the original bricks were scattered around, but we had to make a lot of new mud bricks as well. We were concerned because Mama insisted on helping and even though she was a strong woman who had always worked hard, we men thought this job was too heavy for her. But Mama won and kept helping us until the walls were built.

The Germans did not force us to work on the collective farm, as was the case under communism, but they knew most of the rural population would have to work on these farms as there was very little other work for them. This was the case for us, so Tato, Frossia and I got a job at the collective just down the road, while mother looked after the household. Frossia and I did any work that was needed and Tato looked after the horses. He was known for having a special way with them, although there were not many horses on this farm and they were in very poor condition. We were given very little money and food, however we still had a fair amount of the money left after selling our Terpenia house.

We needed some good strong wood to build a frame around our well, so Tato went looking for some acacia trees which would be perfect for our purpose. He found two good ones and chopped them down, but unfortunately they belonged to a man who had seen Tato taking the wood away. He arrived at our house and angrily told us off, saying he was going to see the village council. Tato was very upset and decided he would also go and speak to the council. When he returned home, he told us that when he and the other man first confronted the council members, they were both very upset. Tato explained to the council that all our trees had been chopped down, even our house had been partly destroyed. The trees were on the border of the two tracts of land and he didn't know that someone else owned them. Even though the councillors were friends of ours, they didn't want to be seen to favour one family over another. They explained that as the land was not owned by farming families but by a collective, which was owned by the Germans, the trees didn't belong to either man. Tato suggested that he give the man some money and when the amount had been agreed upon, everyone seemed satisfied. From that time on our two families became friends.

* * *

We were very pleased to be back in Stepanivka. It was a very beautiful area, very quiet and it had lovely beaches, thus being a favourite spot for town and city folk to spend their holidays. Now that Ukraine was under German occupation, their soldiers also began coming for rest and recuperation. Whole units would arrive, sometimes as many as 200 men, and when one unit left another would arrive. They would barter with the locals and sometimes buy sunflower oil, which they would rub on their bodies before lying on the beach in the sun. Most of the time the place was full of Germans, although none were permanent residents.

Once, when a new unit of German soldiers arrived, they marched through the street outside my home, singing and whistling a very catchy song. I couldn't understand the words and didn't know the name of the song, but the melody stayed in my mind. Many years later I heard it again, this time in English, and remembering how I had liked the song so long ago asked what it was called. I was told that it was a very popular song with both the Germans and British and was called Lili Marlene.

Ivan was still living in Stepanivka. He and his wife hadn't christened their little boy yet and Ivan asked me if I would be the child's godfather. I was pleased to accept but it was so long ago that I cannot recall the child's name. My mother gave me a dozen eggs and 250 grams of butter for the priest in payment for his services, which was my duty as godfather. Money was used for buying larger items, but products were appreciated much more at that time.

We still had some money left over from the sale of the house, so we bought a cow. Most villagers tried to own a cow because having milk, butter and cheese in those difficult times was a big help. We built a small shed attached to the house for the cow in winter. We had owned cows before, but two were taken from us and another was sold for meat as it had stopped giving milk. In summer, the village cows were allowed to graze with the farm cows.

As summer advanced we started to cut the grass which, when dry, would be used as hay for the animals. Everyone helped with the harvesting and I had a chance to work side-by-side with my father. We had to use scythes to do the work. I hadn't used a scythe before so Tato showed me how to handle one. I found it fairly easy. One day I was sharpening my scythe on a stone when I cut my finger fairly deeply. However, it didn't need attention from a doctor and healed quite quickly. When harvesting began, we had to carry on from one crop to the next, as each different crop followed on from the one before. First we cut the grass and left it to dry, turning it over from time to time. When it was dry it would be stacked in a storage shed. Then we would cut the barley and the oats and then the wheat. These cereals would be cut and placed in small stacks, then taken by horse and cart to the harvester for thrashing and later stacked into storage sheds. It was continual work and long hours. But most people enjoyed harvest time.

In autumn the harvest would be finished. The farming families would be given food products for themselves and their animals, which had to last all year. These rations were never enough, especially for the animals. When winter came there were many very dark nights and I would sneak out with a huge fishing net made into a sack to steal hay from the collective farm. I'd carry it on my back and it would have so much hay in it that I would have looked like a small walking haystack if anyone had seen me. I heard that other people did the same thing; if they hadn't the cows would have died of hunger. I don't know if the hay was ever missed. The Germans were as bad as the Soviets, keeping everything for themselves and leaving very little for the workers and their animals.

As we watched our food stocks dwindling, Mama started to worry. One dark night I took a small sack and crept over to the collective farm building where the sweet corn was stored. It was locked, so I found a small nail and tried to pick the lock. To my utter amazement the lock opened and I sneaked inside. I only half-filled the sack because I didn't want to make it obvious that some of the cobs had been taken. I don't think the small amount I took would be missed; the building was huge and packed with sweet corn cobs. I stole from there three more times, when we really needed different food. My parents hated any of us having to steal — they were old-fashioned, honest people — but, under these circumstances, they didn't say anything. What I was doing was dangerous and they worried about me. I would have been in really bad trouble if I had been caught. But it was the Germans, like the Soviets before them, who were the real thieves. This was our country, our land, our soil and we did all the work. When they first warned and threatened us about stealing, they didn't say what the punishment would be. It wasn't difficult to guess that it would be especially unpleasant.

* * *

It was near the end of 1942 when a unit of Kuban Cossacks arrived in our village on leave. They were superb horsemen and rode magnificent horses. Kuban Cossacks originally came from Zaporizhya, but 200 years ago the evil Russian Queen Caterina banished them all to the Kuban district of Russia. They were extremely brave fighters but were always outnumbered and during all those years they kept their Ukrainian identity, customs and language. The Cossacks were billeted in different areas of the village and six of them stayed on our property, pitching tents and cooking their own food. They asked us where they could buy some alcohol. We hadn't started making ours yet, but we knew where large quantities of whisky had been made for commercial use. One of them gave me some money and Mama brought out an empty two-litre bottle. The Cossack gave me his horse, a beautiful slim long-legged chestnut mare, and after I swung into the saddle I had just enough time to grab the bottle before the horse was off like the wind.

Being a country boy I had done a fair amount of riding, but I had never met a horse like this one. I didn't have to touch her with my feet at all. Whichever way I leaned she would go and I only had to pull very gently on the reins for her to stop. When I reached the house to buy the whisky, she stopped with just one light tug, but when I arrived back home and she saw her master she stopped so suddenly I nearly went over her head. 'You're a real Cossack being able to ride my horse,' he said. 'Not everyone would be able to ride a Cossack-trained horse.'

Because Ukraine had been under Russian domination for so long, at first we looked upon the Germans as liberators and these Cossacks were fighting with the Germans against the communists. We heard that in some parts of Ukraine and other Eastern European countries, the people had welcomed the Germans with bread, salt and flowers — a typical Slavic welcome. When the ordinary German soldiers first came to Stepanivka on leave, a few of them were billeted not far from us and we found them quite pleasant. Once or twice we even gave them some borsch. But before very long the Ukrainian people realised the German authorities were just as bad as the Soviets. They kept the collective farms, which meant the people who worked there were still slaves. They sent most of the farm products to Germany and they even took a lot of our soil away in trains. If any soldiers were killed by Russian partisans, the Germans would shoot ten Ukrainians in retaliation for every one of their losses. Sometimes they would also burn the closest village down and there were many cases where the entire village population was wiped out. In some cases they starved whole villages and deliberately burned houses, making the inhabitants homeless in extremely cold weather. It was no use trying to explain the situation to them and, of course, the Soviets didn't mind the killing of innocent Ukrainians at all.

Many German officers were of Russian descent, their ancestors having settled in Germany after World War I. These officers advised the German authorities that Ukrainian numbers must be kept down because they had always wanted independence. So the Germans arrested all the Ukrainian leaders; the intellectuals, such as poets, writers and playwrights, and also priests and any known patriots. Most of them were shot, but there were some who were sent to concentration camps. The same thing had happened when communism began. This had always been Russian policy. When the Germans first invaded the Soviet Union, many Ukrainians refused to fight for their Soviet oppressors and instead surrendered to the Germans, who they thought of as liberators. But the Germans looked upon these Ukrainians as sub-human and treated them in an indescribably evil way. Stalin didn't recognise the Red Cross or the Geneva Convention, so Soviet prisoners received no parcels or any sort of international help. They were just left to their fate. The English-speaking and other prisoners of war were treated reasonably well by the Germans, however millions of Soviet prisoners, most of them Ukrainians, were herded into over-crowded camps. Besides having all the usual precautions against escape, the prisoners were guarded by men with machine guns. They were given almost no food and were forced to live in disgusting conditions. They were sent there to die, and nearly all of them did die of starvation and diseases brought about by malnutrition. In some of the smaller camps, the prisoners would be formed into working parties to do any sort of repairs and also farm work. The Germans needed these people to do the work, so they were fed and treated a little better and a few of them managed to live to see the end of the war.

* * *

Although our family usually made only enough whisky for ourselves and friends who dropped in, when we were preparing for Christmas 1943 we decided to make more, about thirty-five litres. Money was almost useless and when the people from towns and cities arrived, as they did at this time of year, we would barter whisky for shoes and clothing, which we would give each other as Christmas presents. Although we didn't have a lot of food stocks we bartered some of them too, because it was difficult to get food in the towns. I knew that I could steal more food from the collective farm, if necessary; in fact, rob the robbers. We usually made our whisky from sugar beet, although it can be made from wheat, potatoes, sweet corn, apples or almost any fruit or vegetables. It was illegal to make any sort of homebrew but the local police, who were supposed to report any stills they found, liked to have a taste themselves. There were two policemen in our village and they would patrol together. When they walked the village streets they could smell the alcohol aroma in the air and could tell who was brewing. Sometimes they would call at our house. They would rub their hands together and make small talk until Tato asked them if they would like to have a drink with us. They never said no.

Frossia's best friend was called Halya and very soon she became my girlfriend. She was pretty and a very nice person who loved life. She was a very jolly, happy type of person, whereas I was a much shyer and more serious type, but we got on very well. When Christmas arrived we managed to have quite a good party in one of the larger houses. By this time Halya was my steady girlfriend. Our family brought the whisky and some of the young men, myself included, had already sampled some and were quite tipsy. Halya, who was also slightly drunk, put wine in my glass, which already contained whisky. I knew that mixing drinks was silly, but I was too drunk to care. I drank the lot and crashed to the floor like a fallen tree a few minutes later, hitting my head on the table as I fell. I felt terrible and it was so warm in the room that I must have passed out for a short time. Two of my friends, Nick and Mike, picked me up and took me outside where they rolled me in the snow. I felt a little better in the crisp air and although I fully revived I couldn't walk, so they took me under the arms and helped me home. Mama scolded me, telling me I looked like a corpse and to rest for a while. I slept on top of my bed for just over an hour and then felt a lot better, so I went back to the party. When I stepped outside I found that it was a really beautiful night; everything was covered with heavy snow and the air was crisp and cool. There was an enormous full moon and it was as light as day. I could see for miles, and everything seemed to be glistening. I thought what a wonderful painting it would make and tried to keep the picture in my mind. I passed people drinking and singing in the street, and once back at the party I joined my friends and we all had a wonderful time. Everyone got roaring drunk and sang at the top of their voices nearly all night. For a while at least we were able to forget the real world outside.

After the New Year, even though the weather was still very cold, there were quite a few jobs to do. One day around the end of January, I arrived at the collective farm to be told by the supervisor that some of us would work at one of the fishing collectives for a while. He chose a few people, including me. We repaired machinery and fishing nets and I remember cutting sea-ice blocks with a crowbar. The ice was at least twenty centimetres thick and I would pull the blocks out with a hook and load them on to a homemade sledge. Other people would then pull the sledge over ice and land to an enormous hole, which was four metres deep, fifteen metres long and ten metres wide. The loose snow would have to be removed from the hole and the bottom lined with straw before the ice blocks could be put in. Someone would then bring the sledge back to me so I could refill it. When the hole was full it was covered with straw and soil and left until summer, when it was used to preserve the fish. At that time of year I believe the Azov Sea, which was not very deep, was frozen all the way to Kuban, about 300 kilometres away.

Fedor, my nephew, who was only slightly younger than me,

still lived in Stepanivka with his family. We became good friends again, more like brothers than uncle and nephew. We would go to dances and small evening parties. He would take different girls out and Halya and I would often go out with him and his latest girl. Sometimes a group of us, including Frossia, would go out together. One evening Frossia and Halya wanted me to dress up as a girl for a bit of fun. I wouldn't hear of it at first, but eventually they persuaded me. They helped me put on Frossia's dress, scarf and shoes and a little make-up, although girls in those days didn't use much. The girls and my mother thought it was hilarious. It was dusk outside and we thought I might pass if we didn't go where there was too much light. They told me to keep calm and not to laugh; to act shy and walk and talk like a girl.

We walked over to the school grounds, where an outdoor musical evening was in progress. The band was unusual but quite good; there were accordion and mandolin players and two tambourines. Everyone was dancing and having a good time and later there was a joke song, in which anyone could add their own funny words. A boy came over to talk to Frossia and she introduced me as her cousin Ducya from another village. He said, 'What a pretty cousin you have,' and I stood in what I thought was a shy manner, pulling the scarf a little over my face. I spoke in a voice that I hoped sounded female and when we walked, I tried to walk daintily. We all really enjoyed this joke. I didn't do anything to draw attention to myself and after half an hour, I went home. The next day some of the boys asked Frossia about her cousin. Frossia told them Ducya had gone back to her village. The boys said they were sorry to hear that as they had hoped to see more of her! After a while someone told them that it had been me and at first they found it hard to believe, but later thought it was very funny.

Halya and I had become very good friends and we thought we loved each other. I was twenty-one but she was only sixteen. We hadn't been going steady for very long and were not lovers but we decided we would like to get married. I talked to Mama about it. She suggested that as we were both young and there was a war raging, it would be better for us to wait awhile. She said there would still be plenty of time to decide later, after the war. I told Halya what Mama had said and we realised it was sensible advice. It was also our custom for young couples to wait at least two years to be sure they really wished to marry. So we waited. Little did we know that five months later, we would never see each other again.

CHAPTER XI

On guard for the Germans

ONE day in the early spring of 1943 public notices were erected, calling all the young people to a meeting in the council chambers the following Sunday. On the day the German commandant came to speak to us.

Through his interpreter he asked if we wanted to go and work in Germany. He painted a wonderful picture of how life would be — good food, good conditions and plenty of money. We would also be given a free ticket for the journey. He made it sound like paradise but most of us recognised it as propaganda after years of hearing communist lies. If we were interested we had to step forward and register our names. Out of the whole congregation, only four young men agreed to go.

For a while we heard no more about going to Germany, but three weeks later one of the young men who had volunteered arrived home. All four of them had escaped but the other three had been recaptured. I didn't know him, but the whole village soon heard what he had to say. The young men had been sent to work in a factory where the conditions were very poor and their lodgings very cold and over-crowded. They were given very little food of extremely poor quality. Their working conditions were very strict and they had been beaten for even small mistakes. He was sure that the others who had been recaptured would have been severely beaten. I don't know if this man was forced back to Germany or not.

In August the Germans started taking teenage boys and girls away by force. We realised then that they had only been waiting for the year's work to be almost finished. Some people tried to escape from the village before they were taken away. Some were caught and a few got away, but there was nowhere they could go. The Germans had a grip on the whole country and could pick up young people anywhere. Not all the young people from our village were taken, but I was one of those who was. Frossia, Halya and Fedor were left behind.

We were forced to board a train travelling west towards Germany. There were no guards, so when a chance of escape presented itself on the second day, three young men and I took it. As the train slowed going up a steep incline we jumped off, landing safely. Two of the men were from another village and one was from my village. His name was Petro and I only knew him slightly; there must have been about 2000 people in Stepanivka at the time. We all talked for a while before deciding to walk back to our homes. We knew the Germans could send us back again but we thought that they had picked out people at random; there were still young people who were needed to work on the collectives. We hoped we could sneak back into the village and that they would not realise we had been gone. But wherever we went we could be picked up, because it seemed thousands of young people were being sent to Germany.

A week later Petro and I were back in the village doing our usual work. No more people had been taken away, but after two weeks the German commandant came back and sent for Petro and me. He told us through an interpreter that we could be sent to a concentration camp for escaping. However, he said he would give us a chance and that we could choose between a concentration camp and joining a work party, clearing up after the army and repairing things. There was no choice; everyone knew that for a Soviet citizen, concentration camp meant a slow and unpleasant death from starvation. Anyway, I thought I might get a chance to escape later — something that I believed would not be possible from a concentration camp.

* * *

They took us along with a lot of people from other villages by train to a training camp in the Crimean town of Evpatoriya. They taught us how to march, drill and salute. We learnt how to recognise the German ranks because we had to salute the German officers. We were given very old uniforms and old but not-too-bad shoes and putties, which were better than those I had been given in the Soviet army. I realised I was now in the German army and although I didn't like it, it wasn't much different from being forced to work for the other oppressors in the Soviet army. We were taught how to use their rifles, but were only allowed to have one when we were on guard duty. Everyone had to give a password and once when it was my turn on guard duty one man refused to give it. He was messing about but I didn't know this. I thought I might have to shoot him, but at the last minute he said it.

Although we had been tricked into joining the German army, we were allowed to have some time off while we were in training camp, usually at weekends. Petro was also there and we made friends with a few other Ukrainians. When we had some time off we would go into Evpatoriya to a film or pub or just look for girls; there were plenty of willing ones around. After about three months we were taken to the frontline to dig trenches; this was our full-time job.

It was the middle of autumn and the weather was terrible; there was often very cold rain. We could see and hear the Soviet rockets coming over all the time, especially at night. They made a deafening, frightening roar. We could also see the trails of phosphorous from machine gun bullets. We dug trenches at that position for about a week, then were sent to different places to dig more trenches. In a few places we also had to dig bunkers which consisted of one underground room used to shelter from bombardments and air raids. We were only working with spades, picks and our hands, and this work was very hard. We would dig a huge hole, make a roof with timber and then cover it with straw, soil and grass. We had to do the same type of work all the time and it was cold and drizzling rain continuously. We were always hungry, dirty, wet and covered in lice. The soil was getting heavier all the time because the clay held the moisture, and we were also bored by the monotony.

* * *

Once, feeling even more tired, hungry, wet, dirty, lousy and bored than usual, I became so desperate that I did a very foolish thing. I opened the heavy turret of a broken and useless Soviet tank and let the lid fall on my left arm gently a couple of times, dropping it just a little way. I wasn't game to drop it all the way. I realise now that if I had, I would have chopped my arm right off. When my arm became quite swollen, I went to see the German male sister. There was no doctor. I had learnt a few words of German, so I showed him my arm, explaining that I had fallen on the tracks of an abandoned tank. He had a look, but I could see they didn't believe me. However, after attending to it, he gave me two days off.

I spent these days resting on some straw in the shed where we lived. We sheltered in all sorts of different places; sometimes a pigsty, another time a cowshed, anywhere that had a roof. The German catering unit would come round with a mobile kitchen, but we were never given enough food. After my two days off I went back to the sister, who decided that my arm had healed enough for me to go back to work. So I was back at that rotten job that I hated in the cold, wet and dirt. I tried to make the injury flare up again by rubbing it until it looked ugly and inflamed. I also rubbed salt into it, thinking that this would make it worse, not knowing that salt is actually a disinfectant and healer. I went back to the male sister, hoping he would think that it was a reoccurrence of the inflammation. He swore in German, but he did put some ointment and a bandage on it and gave me another day off.

One such ruse that worked involved telling the male sister we were not feeling well and that we thought we had a temperature. He would put a thermometer under our arms and when he wasn't looking, we would flick the thermometer with our thumbnails, sending the mercury up a few degrees. The sister would think the patient was coming down with some illness, and would give him some time off. I managed to get away with this once, but the next time I tried it the sister put the thermometer under my tongue and told me to sit in the waiting room. There were already a lot of men sitting there with thermometers in their mouths, and the sister stood there keeping an eye on us. He warned us that if we tried anything again, he would put the thermometers in a place we wouldn't like — our backsides! He had obviously realised what we were up to.

* * *

The Soviet frontline was only about two kilometres away and it was getting very dangerous. I was fed up with digging trenches in the cold and with everything else, so decided to escape. There were not many options available to me; I didn't even consider going across to the Soviets and I never really wanted to be working for the Germans, so I did a very dangerous and foolish thing. I went further behind the German lines. It was quite dark when I came to a German guard post. I told them that I had lost my company, but of course I didn't say that I was a trench digger or they would have sent me back straight away. Because I boldly walked in and told them, they believed me.

They brought out a motorbike and sidecar. One German rode the motorbike while one sat behind me in the two-person sidecar, holding a short automatic pistol called a Schmeisser. They took me further behind the German lines to a German unit, and were told to take me to a camp where many Soviet stragglers who had been working for them were held until they could be formed into new units.

At the camp, three German officers asked me my name and which unit I had been with. I told them my correct name but gave them the name and number of a unit I knew had been disbanded. They believed me and put me with about twenty other men, an assortment of Ukrainians, Russians, and all sorts of other nationalities who were Soviet citizens. In the evening they put us all in the back of a lorry with a canvas top and a badly worn tin floor. It was fairly dark but we were driving without lights — a normal practice in war time — and there were quite a few Soviet aircraft about.

As well as the men, the lorry was also carrying a forty-four gallon drum of petrol, which was fuel for the lorry. We sat on two long benches facing each other and I was sitting near this drum. After a while we stopped and went into a field to answer the call of nature. When we climbed back in I saw that another young soldier had taken my seat, but I didn't worry because it wasn't too cold near the open back of the lorry where I now sat. About ten minutes later the lorry suddenly slipped off the road and rolled over into a wide drain. We all tumbled on top of each other and I cut both my wrists on the lorry's worn tin floor as I was thrown out the back. We hadn't been going very fast because it was dark, and everyone seemed to be okay, although we all got quite a shock. We had a German medical orderly with us who had a first aid kit, which survived the crash. He was standing quite close to me and even though it was fairly dark he could see by the light of the moon that I was losing a lot of blood. When he realised my wrists were cut he put iodine on them and bandaged them up. He said, 'These cuts are not too bad, though cut wrists can be dangerous.' I understood some German and I knew he was right — the cuts weren't too bad, although I still have scars from them.

Everyone else seemed to be okay, so we looked to see if we could put the lorry back on its wheels. When we peered inside we saw that the forty-four gallon drum had fallen on top of the man who had taken my seat and killed him. I was shocked when I saw the dead man who was sitting in the same seat that I had been sitting in less than fifteen minutes before. I was upset, but not as upset as I would have been had a similar thing happened in peace time. Many terrible things happened all the time, some very suddenly, and we just had to go on. I believe in destiny and decided I had been spared because my time on earth was not yet up.

We left the body in a field at the side of the road — this was not a time to have a proper burial — and between the twenty of us, the two German guards, the medic and the driver, we managed to get the lorry back on the road. We proceeded without further incident to Sebastopol in Crimea, arriving in the early morning. We could hear shells already falling on the outskirts of the town and were shocked to see the terrible mess and destruction the Germans had wreaked in the face of a swift Soviet advance. Lots of beautiful cars of different vintages, lovely furniture and artworks were destroyed in the streets, and they had also taken the barrier from the railway tracks and made new tracks up to the very edge of the cliff. They then pushed cars, trains and train wagons over the cliff, followed by containers of fuel, which were set alight and exploded. None of these things could have been taken with us anyway, because the only way out was by sea and only humans would be going on the ships. Some of the men who could drive rode around the town showing off in the undamaged cars for a couple of hours until the cars had to be destroyed.

Our unit stayed at a big barracks with other units who were already stationed there. German, Hungarian and many other nationalities were gathered together to be moved out by ship. We waited all day for a ship to come in, and when one arrived our unit was put on board the ship with the other units. There must have been at least five or six thousand people on board and the ship was packed. I didn't go with my unit because four other men and I were told to stay behind because there was a bit of cleaning up to be done. We were batmen for the German officers, helping them sort out what small things and personal papers could be taken and what was to be destroyed.

The noise from the frontline was getting louder and we could hear it clearly. Communist partisans had also come down from the mountains to cause trouble, cutting the roads into Sebastopol and making it difficult for anyone to reach the port and escape by sea. On the second day we saw some horse-drawn carts racing to reach the town and on the third day a few more ships arrived. Our ship was a Romanian one and by the time we boarded the ship it was already very crowded, with men from other units and people who had managed to reach the town in front of the advancing Soviets. Most of the civilian population had evacuated the town some time ago but even so, there must have been at least 10,000 men on board. I think this ship may have been the last to leave, because as we pulled away from the docks we could see shells falling on Sebastopol and it looked as if the whole town was in flames. We were already a good distance away when we saw more people racing towards the shore in horse-drawn carts. If, as I believed, this was the last ship, those people were trapped there.

* * *

As we drew further out to sea, a few aircraft started to machine gun us but they didn't drop any bombs. They managed to kill a few people but flew away soon after, which we were thankful for. I think they must have run out of ammunition or were short of fuel. We were so overcrowded we could only stand there helplessly. We had started out in the early morning and by mid-afternoon, we saw a lot of debris; boxes, chairs, tables and many other things floating over a large area of the sea. We didn't see any bodies, but they would have sunk. Obviously a large ship had gone down. I was near the rail waiting, along with hundreds of others, in a queue for the toilet when I heard one of the crew screaming something in Romanian. He was standing on a higher deck and I saw him signal to someone. I saw and felt the ship move slightly off course and as she did, I saw a long black torpedo travelling no more than two metres away from us, just below the surface of the water. It had only just missed us and I could see the white wake it was making. If they hadn't been able to make the slight change in course in time, we would have been blown up and I don't think many people would have survived. Sometimes I still see that torpedo in my mind; it was incredibly close.

We arrived safely at the town of Constanta, in Romania, with no further incident. After we had disembarked, we were taken to a large shed or hangar, where we saw about ten of our mates from our old unit with a few hundred other men, all wrapped in blankets. The ship they had been on, the one I should have sailed on, had been blown up by a torpedo from a submarine. They were the only survivors from about 6000 on board. The debris we had seen must have been from this ship. We heard that a lot of people had drowned because they panicked and tried to pull other people down with them. Also, there were a lot of sharks in the Black Sea.

As soon as it could be arranged, the Germans formed us into small groups and my group was told to walk across Romania towards the Carpathian Mountains where there was an ammunition depot for us to guard. We saw many houses along the way which looked very much like Ukrainian houses; in fact, a lot of Ukrainians had lived in this area of Romania for generations. When we needed to eat and drink we would stop at a village and the Germans would force the village council to give us what we needed.

It was very late autumn but the weather was very good. We came to a small lake, which looked so cool and inviting that we thought we would go in for a dip and have a wash. We all stripped to our underpants and waded into the water but the lake was so shallow that no matter how far we went in, the water was only about thirty centimetres deep. It was also very muddy and we ended up dirtier than before. In fact, we looked like a lot of pigs that had been rolling in mud so we tried to wash by splashing water on ourselves with our hands, but we just stirred up the mud and made it a lot worse.

It wasn't very far to the Carpathian Mountains, just over 250 kilometres, and it took us about two weeks to walk there. We arrived at a small town called Semiorod, meaning "seven towns" because in the olden days, seven small areas had been made into one town. This is an old Ukrainian name, even though we had just crossed the border of Hungary, and there were many Ukrainians who had settled there many centuries ago.

The town was in a valley between two mountains and was surrounded by forest. It was very beautiful. This was our destination and the unit I was in was divided up into smaller units. My group consisted of fifteen men altogether, about half of them German soldiers. The rest of us were Ukrainian, Russian and a sprinkling of other Soviet nationalities.

Our billet was a wooden bungalow-type house, where we were given bunk-type double-story beds. Our job was to guard the ammunition depot, less than half a kilometre away. We were given rifles, bayonets and ammunition and we each had to work in two-hour shifts. There was always two of us on duty together, one on one side of the depot and one on the other, but if anyone had wanted to steal the ammunition it would have been quite easy. Sometimes I would go for a walk in the beautiful country-side, with my rifle of course, but away from the depot, which I shouldn't really have done.

* * *

I was on duty one night at about midnight and it was very dark. I was by myself, sitting on a box of ammunition with my rifle ready, listening carefully because I couldn't see even a short way in front of me. At first it was just a calm dark night, but then I heard the crunch of footsteps close by. I was nervous. I knew there were dangerous wild pigs in the area, and I told myself it could be a goat or a rabbit, but what if it was partisans? They were well trained in guerilla warfare and could sneak up and kill me. I became more nervous imagining things, and the footsteps seemed to be getting closer and closer. I was very frightened and squeezed the trigger of my rifle. It made an absolutely deaf-ening reverberating sound in the valley on such a quiet night. I was surprised how loud it sounded. Five or six guards came running from the watch house. I told them something very big was crashing its way through the forest so I had shot at it. Using torches, they looked around everywhere and couldn't find a thing. Whatever it was had got away. I had shot wildly in the dark and obviously hadn't hit anything, but nobody complained and after a while they all went back to bed. Afterwards I thought it must have been a goat because there was too much noise for a rabbit, wild pigs make more noise and the partisans would cer-tainly be more professional than to make that sort of noise. But for quite a while I had to put up with teasing and ribbing about being frightened of a rabbit.

When I first came to the ammunition depot the German authorities had asked me my name and nationality. The next day they gave me a blue and yellow cloth badge with an emblem on it and I was told to sew it on to the left sleeve of my battle jacket. I could see that the emblem was made up of Ukrainian letters but I didn't know what it meant. A few days later, after I had finished guard duty, I decided to walk into Semiorod. On the way I met an elderly Ukrainian civilian who had lived all his life in that part of Hungary, near the Carpathian Mountains. We started talking and I asked him what the emblem on my arm stood for. He told me that the blue and yellow were the colours of the Ukrainian flag — blue for the sky and yellow representing cornfields or sunflowers. The emblem was called a *Tryzub*. He told me the O in the middle of the emblem was the first letter in the name of Queen Olga, who was the first Ukrainian royal to embrace Christianity. The letters on each side of the O stood for Queen Olga's son, Prince Vladimir, and her grandson, Prince Yerislav, both of whom later became kings of Ukraine. When Vladimir became king, he brought Christianity to all Ukraine.

Because I had been born and spent a lot of my life in south-eastern Ukraine I had never heard any of this; everything patriotically Ukrainian had been deliberately kept from us by our Russian occupiers. I hadn't even known that blue and yellow were the colours of the Ukrainian flag.

* * *

We were allowed to walk into Semiorod quite often. One day in early winter, three young Ukrainians and I decided to go in to the town. We earned a very small amount of money, so we thought we would look around the town and do a bit of shopping. As we approached the outskirts of the town, we saw a large, very beautiful house. It looked deserted, although it wasn't damaged. The front door was wide open and there was no one about, so we decided to have a look around. Inside, it was big and beautiful, with huge windows and very expensive-looking green curtains. The furniture was big and heavy and had a lovely reddish sheen. There was an enormous fireplace and lots of paintings and fine clocks on the walls. I had never seen such a magnificent place. We just walked around admiring the place and looking up at the fancy ceiling and small chandeliers.

On the floor were a few boxes of fancy buttons which looked like they were part of someone's collection. They were open and the buttons were scattered over the floor with cutlery and other small items. Someone who had been there before us had been looking for anything small of value, but there was nothing that would be of any value to us. Everything was very fine but too big and we couldn't use any of the smaller things as we lived in the ammunition depot lodgings. We couldn't see any food, drink or smokes, but before we could look for a cellar we heard the noise of aircraft overhead. We ran into the garden where we had seen a shallow trench, which must have been used as an air raid shelter. We stood in the trench and watched two Soviet aircraft machine-gunning the roof of a nearby church. They must have thought it was being used as an observation post. One of the heavy-calibre bullets went very wide, missing the church and whizzing past my face by a mere hair's breadth before slamming into the wall of the trench.

The planes finally left, and although no one had been hit my heart was beating a lot faster after that near miss. We went into the town, where we were told by the townsfolk that earlier, it had been machine-gunned by the same two aircraft and that quite a few people had been killed or injured. We didn't feel like looking around anymore, so we bought some fruit and walked back to our billet. We avoided the house on the way back.

CHAPTER XII

Escape

WE had been at the ammunition depot for about two months, when we began hearing very loud thunderous sounds in the distance. The frontline was creeping closer and closer.

I began to feel very unwell. I was short of breath and had a pain in my chest. I could also hear noises coming from my chest. I told my commanding officer who sent me into town to see a German army doctor. It wasn't far, so I walked. After examining me, the doctor handed me some papers and told me to go back to the depot. He told me to give the papers to my commanding officer and said, 'I will also phone him.' I walked back and when my CO read the papers he told me to pack my things and walk back to Semiorod's railway station, where hospital trains were arriving and departing all the time. When I arrived I had to show the special pass my CO had given me to the stationmaster, then after waiting just half an hour a hospital train arrived from the Eastern front. The beds were in tiers; I was given one of the top ones.

I slept for a while and in the early afternoon looked down to see a bag belonging to one of the soldiers lying open on one of the lower beds. I could see a browning pistol with a red star on it and a very good pair of binoculars. I knew that the person, probably a German, had souvenired them. I would very much have liked to souvenir them from him — it was the binoculars I fancied, not the gun — but there was nowhere to hide them, and if I'd been caught I would have been in real trouble. I didn't really want to steal from the sick and wounded and anyway, most of the troops on the train were Germans and they would have killed me if I'd taken their property.

It wasn't very far to the town where the hospital was — only one day's train journey — and I was transferred to an ambulance with five others and driven to a hospital about eighty kilometres from Vienna, Austria, set in a very beautiful forest. I was put in a ward with quite a few other men, then we were given food — very nice pork sausages with vegetables and potatoes in their skin. This was the first time I had eaten potatoes in their skin and I tried to take the skins off. Someone said, 'Eat the skins, they're good for you,' but I thought it was rather like the food we had given to our animals. But the potatoes were clean and oven-baked and didn't taste too bad at all. The bread was quite dark and seemed mixed with something else but that tasted good too. It was nice to have a good substantial meal for a change.

A sister put a hot, wet poultice on my chest. I think it was a mustard poultice because it was very hot and felt like sandpaper. It was taken off half an hour later. In four hours another one was applied then taken off and we went through this procedure for two days. I was asleep when the German doctor visited four days later. He and some nurses walked around the ward talking to the patients. They woke me up and asked how I felt. I was grumpy because I had been woken so I said I felt terrible and that I wasn't getting any medicine or treatment, except the poultices, and even that had stopped. I am sure I said the wrong thing because a couple of days later I was discharged from the hospital. They couldn't find my uniform so they gave me another one. It didn't have a *Tryzub*, which I really wanted now that I knew what it meant.

I was put on a train with a few other men and sent to a large camp in a small town called Noyhammer, which I think was near Dresden. It was a camp of stragglers who had been disbanded or lost their units, or who had just come out of hospital. We were billeted in a wooden bungalow-type building and were given those double storey-type bunk beds again. We were supposed to be formed into new units, but we were forced to become slaves for the farmers. We had to pick potatoes and swede-type turnips, which we ate raw if we were hungry. We usually were. I didn't like the turnips and we already had them cooked as food in the camp, so everyone was fed up with them. Even today I still don't like them and they are the only food I really won't eat.

The remnants of a Ukrainian division, which had been fighting the communists on the Eastern front, were also in the camp. Half the division had been killed or taken prisoner, or they had joined the Ukrainian insurgent army. Kuban Cossacks were camped there with their families, and had horses, machine guns and some heavy equipment. They had been fighting Tito's communists in Yugoslavia, but were outnumbered and overwhelmed. Tito's partisans took no prisoners and killed men, women and children. Those who managed to escape came to that camp at Noyhammer.

We slaved for the farmers for about a month, after which we were split into units of about 130 men. My unit was sent by train to Northern Italy, where we joined a German division before settling in a small town near the larger town of Modena. As much as I hated working for those farmers, I was feeling a lot better; the outdoor work picking vegetables had been a great help and the mustard poultices might have helped too.

* * *

It was the beginning of 1944 and the war was going against the Germans. I was pleased about this — I'd never liked being forced to work for them, so when some other Ukrainians in the German unit suggested we join the Italian partisans, I decided to try it.

The partisans were dangerous, but treated you okay if you joined them and they were in touch with the Americans stationed on the other side of the mountains. This was why I decided to join them. The partisans knew a way across the mountains and by travelling along the partisans' passage we could avoid the front line. Although we wore German uniforms and were billeted in their houses the Italian townspeople, who hated the Germans, knew we were from other countries so were friendly to us. We would drink wine with them in the cafes and eventually some of them told us how to find the partisans operating in the area.

My first really good chance to escape came a few days later, and although it was risky, I went on my own and didn't tell anyone. The locals had told us to go outside the town and start walking down a certain small country road, so I made my way there in search of the partisans. There was very little to see, just fields of grass and walls made of rounded stone, and I walked about three kilometres before I saw a cottage. I was about to approach when I heard the sound of engines from down the road. I jumped over a small wall and hid just as a lorry-load of German soldiers drove past. They were moving so quickly they didn't even see me. I made my way to the cottage and knocked on the door. It was opened by a farmer and his wife, both middle-aged, and inside I saw a very beautiful young girl of about eighteen. She must have been their daughter. I couldn't speak Italian very well, but I said the words "mountains" and "Americans" and they seemed to get the idea. They asked me inside and gave me some food — dark bread and something like cooked grass, which was slightly bitter. The girl brought me a towel and bowl of water so that I could wash my hands and face, and a bottle of wine in a straw container and a glass. I sat down to eat and the father went out, saying he would bring some partisans to me.

As I ate I couldn't take my eyes off the girl. She had long black hair, a lovely face and a very nice figure. She was very attractive. The older woman, who I'm sure was her mother, saw me staring and told me to keep away from the girl because she had a dreadful disease. I understood and realised she was saying this to protect her daughter from a foreign soldier who might harm her. We all tried to carry on a conversation while we waited for the father to return. I began to get a bit worried after a few hours, for all I knew the farmer had gone to the Germans.

It was almost dark when the man finally returned with five heavily-armed men, who I discovered were partisans. They stared at me, guns pointed at my chest, and I felt very nervous standing there in my German uniform. One of them searched me for weapons and another spoke to me in Russian. I told him I was Ukrainian even though he insisted I was Russian. I could speak Russian well, having lived most of my life in the Russian-occupied part of Ukraine. I told him I wanted to join the partisans, travel over the mountains and possibly meet up with the Americans. After relating quite a bit of my story he decided that I was okay. The partisan band gave me a handgun and told me I was now a member of the Garibaldi Brigade, Garibaldi being a hero to some of the Italian people. The farmer gave me some trousers and a jacket, which I put on over my uniform, and a cap. It would be very cold when we crossed the mountains, but I didn't care; at last I was taking a step towards joining up with the Americans.

There was an Italian woman with the partisans, who looked and dressed like a young man. When the Russian member told the Italians that I too was Russian, she asked me the Russian word for breasts, indicating that area of her body. I told her the word and added that I had seen better ones. The Russian must have translated this accurately because everyone laughed. We walked into the night for about a kilometre, then turned off the road onto a small track. We walked for another two hours until we came to a small shed at the foot of the mountains where ten other men were waiting for us. They too wanted to get to the American camp on the other side of the mountains.

We continued for about another five hours, gradually climbing up, and it became cooler as we rose, with the air quite misty around us. We could only just manage to see the way. We were quite high up the mountain when we came to a shepherd's hut, which was also used by mountain climbers in peacetime. There was a fireplace, some dry wood, a pan and water. There were also some bags of powdered chestnuts, which we used to make a thick pudding that was naturally sweet. We slept on some straw for about four hours before setting off again.

I felt quite well, no chest trouble, and I think the mountain air helped me. We climbed for about another three hours before reaching the mountain peak and were able to rest for a while before going down the other side. It was a long way down, even if it was easier than going up. At the bottom was a shallow river with icy cold water and a bed of small boulders. It was running very swiftly and was quite narrow, so we took off our socks and boots and waded across. We dried our feet, put our socks and boots back on and headed up the next mountain. This one was very high; we climbed up and up and were soon in the clouds. Sometimes loose stones went rolling down the face of the mountain, and while we couldn't see where they went, we could hear the noise of them falling. They seemed to go on and on forever.

We kept going for most of the day and very late into the night before we finally came to another hut, where ten more partisans were waiting. They'd had a skirmish with a German patrol; there were three German bodies outside. One of the partisan leaders had been shot in the stomach and was still alive, so we stayed there for a few hours while the men tended him and dressed his wounds. They had made a stretcher with blankets and pieces of wood and told us to carry him down the mountain. I was one of the first four picked to carry the stretcher — one person for each corner.

Carrying this man was very heavy work. He moaned and cried most of the time and sometimes, when we slipped on the loose stones, his body would hit the track. Another four took the stretcher after half an hour and we swapped back and forth every thirty minutes until, about four hours later, the poor man died. It was a relief for him, and for us also. As soon as we could, we stopped and buried him in a shallow ditch; it was too rocky to dig a real grave. The Italians made a wooden cross from tree branches and carved some words on it with a knife. They said some prayers before we moved on.

In the next days we crossed mountains and valleys and very cold streams. There seemed to be so many mountains that I lost count, but I think there must have been six in all. We discovered that people lived in some of the valleys, and there were a few farms where the people kept sheep, goats, cows and donkeys. The farmers gave us food: polenta pudding, which is made of ground sweet corn, cheese, bread and milk. Others gave us bread, milk, a bitter vegetable, and other cooked vegetables. Sometimes we were given wine or dried figs, which the people grew themselves. The valleys were quite fertile. More people joined us along the way and by the time we had crossed the last mountain, there was quite a crowd of us. At the start of my journey I had been alone but at the end there must have been at least sixty people in total.

CHAPTER XIII

Tiger hunters

A FTER a week of walking over mountains and valleys we found ourselves in a large town called Pistoia. I had been wondering what the Americans would look like and when a patrol came past in two jeeps, I saw that three of them were black like Paul Robson, whom I had seen many years ago. The rest looked just like us. They stopped, and after the Italians explained who we were, they told us to follow them. The jeeps drove slowly as we walked behind them and soon we arrived at an American camp. An American officer spoke to us through an Italian interpreter. He told us to surrender our weapons, so those of us who had weapons put them down on the ground. Then he asked any Soviet citizens to step forward and I was surprised that there were so many of us. Not all were Ukrainian or Russian, but were from different areas of the Soviet Union.

All those who stepped forward were taken to a different camp a short distance away, where about 100 other Soviet men were housed. We were there for a week before they took us to the port city of Livorno, where we were put straight on board a ship bound for Naples. It took two days to reach Naples, where we went straight from the ship to a passenger train headed for Taranto in Southern Italy. In Taranto there was quite an international reception committee — Americans as well as other people with badges on their arms which I managed to interpret as Canadian. I think the British were also there — they looked how I thought the British would look — plus a few Italian policemen. But a jolt of fear

shot through me when I saw some officers who looked horrify-
ingly like Soviets. I felt frozen with dread and a chill wind blew
right through my body. I thought that if they forced us to go back
I'd go mad and shoot them all, except the Americans had taken my
gun. I loved my country more than words can tell, but nothing on
earth could make me want to return to the Soviet Union. I loathed
the communist regime and since I escaped from the Germans I
had hoped to somehow stay in Italy, or possibly even America.

But there was no escape this time. After being forced to march
about three kilometres to a Soviet repatriation camp on the
outskirts of a large town, the authorities registered and interro-
gated us. They wanted to know our names, home addresses and
everything that had happened to us since we had left the Soviet
Union. I asked what would happen if I didn't want to go back but
they said I had no choice — I was a Soviet citizen and therefore
required to help rebuild the Fatherland. I insisted that I did not
want to return, but they just laughed at me.

There were thousands of men in this camp living in small canvas huts housing up to ten people each. However, I was put under
guard in a special isolated area surrounded by barbed wire. My
hut was the same as the others, but I shared with only one other
man. He was also a Ukrainian, from the western part of the country, which had been under Polish rule. He was also under arrest
because he had told the Soviet authorities that he was a Polish
citizen, not a Soviet citizen, which was why he was in this area
away from the others.

There was always an armed guard stationed just outside the
barbed wire, near a small gate, and we were not allowed into
the main camp. Because we were prisoners food was brought to
us — we were not allowed to go into the kitchen. Unfortunately
we were not so isolated that we couldn't hear the loud speakers,
placed at intervals around the camp, broadcasting the news and

constantly telling us about the ferocious battles our glorious Red Army had won. We were bombarded with political propaganda — especially about Stalin being our beloved father who would forgive us for all we had done since leaving the Soviet Union. He was our "wonderful teacher" and the war's "greatest strategist", as well as being a genius — almost a god. It was our patriotic duty to return to our Fatherland and to help rebuild our shattered homes and country, because we were all one big happy family.

Some of the men were enthusiastic about going back to the Soviet Union and indeed looked forward to boarding a ship which apparently would be ready to sail to Odessa, Ukraine's largest seaport, in a few days. Most of these men were from the young communist movement and they believed this propaganda. They would march around the camp, waving red flags and singing patriotic Soviet songs. I didn't know then that Stalin was the worst war criminal the world has ever known and that he was even worse than Hitler, because most of Hitler's atrocities had already been committed by Stalin. But I did know how much my people and country had suffered under the communist regime and although I didn't know how I was going to manage it, I knew I could never return to the Soviet Union. I heard much later that everyone who was forced back home was either killed or given at least ten years in some sort of jail. People were punished for having seen how much better things were in countries outside the USSR and were kept locked away, so they could not tell anyone else. I also heard that men who had walked home from the frontline for the same reason I had, and were still in their villages when the communists returned, were forced by the NKVD to become unarmed human shields for the Soviet soldiers as they advanced to meet the Germans. Those who were not killed by the Germans were shot in the back by the NKVD, who brought up the rear.

* * *

One of the guards, an Asian, was quite a pleasant person and when he was on duty we used to talk. He was a Muslim from Kazakhstan in Central Asia and had been in this camp longer than most. He said that a ship had sailed a couple of weeks ago from Taranto to Odessa and people who didn't want to go back had jumped from the ship into the sea. Some had drowned and others were picked up and brought back to this camp. He didn't know if anyone had managed to escape but those who were brought back told him that, once out to sea, there was no more propaganda or soft talk. The prisoners were considered hardened criminals and were treated very badly indeed. The crew had told them that people on an even earlier voyage had tried to escape by jumping into the open sea near Greece. The ones who had been brought back onboard had been imprisoned in the hold, chained and treated worse than slaves of olden times.

The Ukrainian who shared my hut was a nice middle-aged man called Roman. I can't remember his other names. He would have liked to have stayed in Italy but couldn't decide what to do, because he had a wife and two children back home. In the end he decided to go back, but before he went he wanted to help me escape. Roman told me there were many units of the Polish army in Italy, but that the Poles were under the overall control of the British and wore British uniforms with "Poland" written on the arm badge. They would take Ukrainians in the Polish army and suggested I try to reach them. I didn't speak any Polish so he taught me a few words. He also suggested I change everything about myself; my name, date of birth, religion and all other particulars. He gave me a new Polish name — Stanislaw Wilsanski — and told me to say my parents were from Crakow in Poland, but that they had moved to Kharkiv in Ukraine after the revolution.

He suggested that I say my parents had died in 1933 and the reason I couldn't speak much Polish was because I was brought up in a children's home where only Ukrainian and Russian had been spoken.

* * *

Once I had my story straight, all we had to do was think of a way for me to escape. The only way would be through the gate — the rest of the area was surrounded by barbed wire. I chose to try to get past the Asian guard whom we knew slightly. I had 200 lire and Roman gave me another 100 (about fifteen shillings in total). I was to show the money and a homemade water container to the guard and ask if I could nip out to buy some wine from the farmhouse, in full view of our hut and about half a kilometre away. So, when this guard next came on duty, I showed him the can and the money and said, 'How about letting me just nip out to that farmhouse and get some wine?' He refused, but I badgered him several times, saying, 'Look, it's less than half a kilometre, I'll be back before anybody knows I've gone and you can have some of the wine.' (He drank wine, even though he was a Muslim and shouldn't have done so.) In the end, he let me go — I still can't believe he did. He must have known why we were in that compound and why we were being guarded. He should have known there was a good chance we would try to escape and that he would be in terrible trouble if we succeeded.

I strolled in the direction of the farmhouse, keeping to the middle of the road, swinging the container as if I was only thinking about wine. I didn't want Roman and the guard to get into trouble, but how could I let this opportunity to escape pass by without trying? Roman wanted me to escape and I believe that he gave me the plans he had thought out for himself. As I approached the farm I passed through a lot of fruit trees and bushes and went round to the back of the house. I then threw the container away and ran towards some hills I could see in the distance. It was early evening and quite dark, so I stopped running when I reached a forest, then walked as fast as I could to the top of a small hill. I looked back and saw the camp all lit up about three kilometres away and more lights from the town of Taranto further away. I said a loud goodbye and started to walk across a plateau thick with trees. I had no idea where I was going, so decided to travel north — the direction away from the camp. I walked all night. I couldn't see very well so I walked with my arms out in front of me and I could just see the stars above the treetops. I wasn't moving very fast, but at least I was moving.

In the morning I came to a poor-looking farmlet. The house was made of stone and there was a field of grapevines. A dog barked loudly and an elderly Italian farmer came out and stood looking at me. I asked for some bread and water and he gave me some dark bread, some cooked bitter vegetable, a bottle of wine in a straw container and a glass on a small tray. I sat on a large rock and ate the breakfast he had provided while he sat on another rock nearby. He asked where I was going and I replied, 'north'. He said, 'Yes, yes you escaped,' so he knew where I had come from. When I finished eating he gave me some tobacco (I still smoked in those days). He also gave me a linen bag containing bread and cheese. I would have liked to pay him as he seemed quite poor, but when I tried to give him money he wouldn't take it. So I thanked him instead and he told me to continue north to the city of Barry. He managed to tell me to get the train from there by making train noises and arm movements. My Italian wasn't very good, but I understood him.

Just before midday I came to the railway line on the outskirts of Barry. I noticed two goods trains standing in a siding, one of which was pointing in the right direction and looked almost ready to depart. Some of the wagons were carrying large pieces of coal, and one truck was only half full so I pulled myself up and sat on the coal out of sight. After about half an hour the train started to move. It travelled through Barry and for about 200 kilometres before stopping at a very small seaside railway station. It was almost evening and as it was quite a while since I had eaten, I decided it was time I looked for more food and drink and somewhere to sleep.

I went down the water's edge, dusted my clothes the best I could and washed my hands and face. There were a few houses behind the station so I decided I would try to buy food with my Italian money. I knocked on the door of the last house and when a middle-aged man opened it, I asked him if I could buy some food. He asked me in and spoke quickly to his family — his wife and teenage son and daughter. He took me outside and showed me the water pump where he washed his hands. I washed mine too, even though I had just washed them in the sea.

It was obvious that the family was just about to eat supper and they asked me to eat with them. The woman had made spaghetti, which they all covered with grated cheese and tomato sauce. I had never eaten this long thin type of pasta before so I watched them and followed their lead. At home we had always used the shorter noodle type in soup or milk puddings. They gave me a spoon and fork but I had a difficult time eating the spaghetti, which fell everywhere. I was starting to get embarrassed because everyone was watching me and then the whole family roared with laughter. I couldn't help but join in. The father showed me how to eat the spaghetti, putting it on the fork and rolling it around while holding the spoon underneath. After that I managed to get it in my mouth and they kept putting more and more on my plate. It was very nice food and I was very hungry. And the Italian family seemed to enjoy me enjoying it.

We all had a glass of wine and then I tried to pay them. They wouldn't take money, but the father asked if I would do some work for them the next day. I couldn't grasp what they wanted doing, but said I would work for the food and be happy to do so. I slept on the kitchen floor because they didn't have much room, and I was very grateful for this. It was warm and comfortable and they gave me plenty of blankets. I was full of spaghetti and wine and very tired from my journey, and as soon as I lay down on the floor I fell asleep. I had rid myself of my German uniform at the American camp and had been wearing the Italian worker clothes given to me by the farmer with the lovely daughter at the start of my trek over the mountains.

* * *

When I woke the next morning I washed at the pump and went back to the kitchen where the farmer's wife prepared breakfast for us. We had bread, cheese and tea. We then went out into the field where they had seedlings of carrots, lettuce, beans and onions which needed weeding. The farmer, his son and I used hoes and worked quite hard until almost midday. As meal time approached we put our tools away and went up to the house. The farmer's wife had made a very nice soup with meat and vegetables and macaroni. Again we finished our meal with a glass of wine. We then rested for about an hour.

My hair was very long and the farmer asked if I would like to go to the barber for a haircut. I said I would, and on the way he explained that he had told the rest of the village people about me. There were so few houses that I wouldn't have called it a village. There were quite a few men waiting for the barber, but when they saw me they stood back to let me go first. I sat in the barber chair while he snipped at my hair, then I happened to look up at the opposite wall. There was a large picture of Stalin hanging there. It was a terrible shock — I was quite stunned and felt chilled. These people who had been so good and kind to me must've been communists. I felt sure they didn't know what communism was really like. I didn't say anything, just sat there quietly and allowed the barber to finish cutting my hair. I tried to pay him, but he wouldn't take any money, so I thanked him and the farmer and prepared to leave. While I sat in the barber's chair I had listened to the Italians arguing and realised they were disagreeing about what to do with me. One man said he would take me to the British post and I agreed to this — I didn't have any other plans. But I started to worry when, in the reflection of the barber's mirror, I saw one of the customers give a small hand gun to the man who was to accompany me. I hoped he wasn't going to shoot me once we got away from this hamlet.

After about two kilometres we came upon a railway line. There was a small house there and a jeep standing outside. Inside there were two English soldiers who seemed friendly, so my companion spoke to them then left to go back to his hamlet. The soldiers motioned for me to sit down and offered me some tea, but I couldn't understand what they meant. *Ti* in my language means "you". *Chi* is the word for tea in Ukrainian. "Tea" is the first English word I ever remember hearing. They poured a cup for me and to my utter astonishment, poured milk into it! This was the first time I had seen anyone put milk in tea and I was surprised to find that it tasted quite good. They poured some tea for themselves and brought out a plate of biscuits, so we all enjoyed a snack. One of the soldiers then made a telephone call.

A few hours later, a British jeep carrying two soldiers pulled up outside. Both soldiers carried rifles, but I didn't worry too much because it seemed normal that soldiers should be armed in wartime. They gestured me into the jeep and took off the way they had come. As we sped along the country road I couldn't help thinking — hoping — that perhaps now I would have the chance to live in another country. After two hours we stopped outside a small camp surrounded by a high wire fence, which I later found out was the international camp in Barry. Inside the fence, the British soldiers handed me over and an American officer showed me the dining room and the barracks where I would sleep. I met some of my fellow inmates and discovered there were people from many different countries temporarily housed at the camp.

Two days later a rumour went around that the "tiger hunters" were coming. This is what the Soviet repatriation mission officers were called by the Soviet citizens they were hunting. This news was terrifying to us and I was horrified, scared and very angry. I had gone through a lot to get this far and now I seemed to be back to where I started. Sure enough, three Soviet officers arrived at the camp shortly afterwards. They had lots of gold braid on their shoulders and were walking around the camp escorted by some American officers. I panicked and along with about ten other Soviet citizens, crawled through a hole in the fence at the far end of the camp, behind some barrack huts. The hole had obviously been made by other people thinking to escape. We hid behind some bushes while the officers scoured the camp for Soviet citizens and as soon as they left, we climbed back through the hole. Later we were told that when the officers looked around and made enquiries, they couldn't find one Soviet citizen. I often think about that hole in the fence. If I had known where to go I probably would not have crawled back inside the camp perimeter. But I also hoped the Americans might help me settle in a country outside the Soviet Union, now that the Soviet officers had been and gone.

The following day the American commandant told us, through interpreters, that if we wanted to stay out of prison and wanted to eat we had to be registered, giving our names and all other details. I was called to the office and when asked my name and country of origin I said, 'Ivan Holly from Czechoslovakia.' *Holly* in Ukrainian means "naked", which was how I felt. A day later some of us were summoned to the office by loudspeaker. They called Ivan Holly so I went to the office where I found the American commandant and another man in American uniform who spoke to me in Czech. I understood enough to have a conversation with him, but not nearly enough to pass as a bona fide Czech. He said to me, 'You are not Czech — you're Ukrainian, a Soviet citizen.' There was no way out for me, so I spoke to him in my language, telling him how much I didn't want to go back to the USSR. I also told him some of my story and asked if he could help me. He sympathised and said he would do his best. I told him I wanted to work for the Americans if they could help me get to any other country, but he said it wasn't up to him. He would, however, put a good word in for me with the commandant, who would probably speak to the American authorities.

I went back to my barracks and waited. About nine am the next day, my name and a few others were called over the loudspeaker. We went to the main office where the commandant and an American captain came in. The captain spoke to us in several different languages telling us to go and sit in the lorry parked outside. Two American Negro soldiers with automatic weapons sat with us. We had no idea where they were taking us and I thought, *we're in trouble*. The soldiers looked like guards and it seemed as if the Americans, too, were treating us as sub-humans and of no importance.

We drove for about three hours before I noticed from the back of the lorry that the places we were passing seemed familiar. In fact I was sure that the area was Taranto, the town near the Soviet camp I had recently escaped from. My heart sank and I felt terrified; doomed. I couldn't escape from the lorry — I would never get past the American guards with their automatic weapons. Beneath my despair I couldn't understand why the Americans, and I suppose the British, would be doing this — forcing people back to where they didn't want to go. They must have had some idea of what communism was like. Why wouldn't they give those of us who wanted to get away a chance?

I found out many years later that an agreement had been signed in Yalta by Churchill, Roosevelt and Stalin, which authorised the forced repatriation of Soviet citizens by the Americans, British and French. I was told many of the allied soldiers didn't like doing this but were under orders. Under the agreement, the Russians would help the other three countries with the return of their servicemen. I was told and also read that many people killed themselves rather than be returned to the USSR. A lot of the Kuban Cossacks who had been fighting in Yugoslavia committed suicide rather than be handed back to the communists. The Allied Command, most of the Soviet citizens, and even the allied soldiers knew or had a very good idea what would happen to these people. I was told later that one group of people who had been handed over to the communists were shot, right in front of the people who had given them up. I don't believe the allies expected that.

CHAPTER XIV

What price freedom?

W HEN the lorry finally came to a halt, my worst fears were confirmed. It was the same camp. I had travelled in a huge circle and was back at the same Taranto camp I had escaped from. I thought, *this is the end of me.*

Three Soviet officers came out of the office and the American officer gave one of them some papers. None of these Soviet officers were ones I had seen before. I felt like a stray animal — the Americans had given us up. One of the Soviet officers looked at the papers and walked along the line, speaking to each man. When he came to me he said, 'Ivan Holly?' I replied, 'Yes.' He asked me if I had escaped from this camp, to which I replied no. He called me a liar but I said, 'No, I'm not, this is my first time here.'

I joined a unit of fifty men who occupied one section of the camp. I was shown to a canvas hut, which was already occupied by six others. We all walked together to the kitchen tent where we were given thick stew, bread and fruit. We were allowed to take the food back to our hut and as we walked back, I imagined that people in the distance were watching me, but nobody bothered me. Some of the men ate outside, but I decided to eat inside just in case anyone recognised me. However, I was starting to think that the people who had been here before had been shipped home. So far I had seen nobody who looked familiar.

The leader of my hut told me that most of the people in the camp were going to the movies that evening, about a kilometre away. I decided to go with them — I was already looking for an opportunity to escape. We had to march in columns to the picture house, which was a large hut with hard chairs. Naturally, it was a Soviet film and just a whole lot of propaganda. I watched for a while but soon got fed up. During the interval, when the lights went up, I looked around and saw some officers two rows behind me, one of which I recognised as having been in the camp when I was there before. I sank down in my seat and when the lights went off and the movie started again, I slowly got up and made for the exit. Nobody stopped me. I went outside and around to the back of the cinema hut as if I was going to the toilet.

I looked around but no one was in sight — I was surprised that I had been allowed outside by myself and wasn't going to waste the opportunity. I edged further away and came to some olive trees, passing through them to a large open field. On either side of me I could see brightly lit camps about two kilometres away. I was standing directly between the two of them. I had no idea what sort of camps they were and couldn't take the chance of being seen, so I crawled across on my hands and knees. There was no cover of any sort. I crawled for what seemed like kilometres, but was possibly only a few hundred metres. The grass and small stones were very sharp and I was cut and scratched on my arms, legs and face — even my stomach. But it was worth it if I could escape from that camp.

After a while the ground began sloping downwards, like a small valley. I could see small clumps of high grass so I started to run in a crouching position. Soon I came to more trees and was able to walk normally. There were a lot of trees and the ground began to slope upwards, and I realised I was in the same high country as the first time I had escaped. I walked north again along a small but well-made country road through the forest. I found a shed with a bit of hay inside and laid down to rest. There were quite a few mice, but they didn't bother me and I slept well.

* * *

I awoke to a clear, fine day and started walking again. I couldn't help thinking that if these camps had been in the Soviet Union it would not have been so easy to escape. There would have been barbed or electrical wire surrounding the grounds and also towers or platforms with armed guards. But in Italy the Soviets obviously didn't want to show their true colours. And, as the allies were rounding up the Soviet people for them, it was my guess that the communists got most of their victims back. I wondered what had happened to Roman, and decided that he must have gone back to Ukraine.

As I walked along I saw a farmlet which had many rows of grapevines with rows of wheat growing between them. It was too close to the camp so I didn't stop. After a while I came to a large country road. A few people passed by but took no notice of me. I suppose I looked like a peasant in my Italian working-style clothes and I was also pretty grubby, as someone going home from work might be. I walked for two days, stopping at farms to ask for food. The ones who gave me food wouldn't take any money and the others told me to go to the village shop because they couldn't spare anything. Naturally I wanted to keep away from towns and villages if I could manage to do so.

On the third day I had to pass through a small town, and as I walked along a street I saw four soldiers in British uniforms. On their left sleeves were cloth tags with "Poland" written in English. I wanted to speak to them but was too scared, not knowing what would happen if I approached them. I kept walking until I saw a workshop for repairing army lorries. There were six lorries outside and the drivers, who also had Poland tags, were standing around. I was desperate, so went up to them and spoke in Ukrainian. One of them answered me in Russian. He also spoke

Polish and said something to the other men, then started speaking to me again. I told him only a little of my story, being wary of everyone. I told him I wanted to join the Poles and get a job with them, either as a soldier or civilian. He said he couldn't help me, but there were a lot of Ukrainians in the Polish units of the British army. He told me to go to the next town and gave me some white bread. It seemed very white, like cotton wool — I hadn't seen white bread for years. He also gave me a tin of corned beef and some cigarettes, which he took from the back of one of the lorries. He wished me good luck and sounded as if he meant it. Then he told me some news that rocked me. The war was over. The allies had taken Berlin and the Germans had capitulated.

I walked in a daze towards the town as the soldier had directed and soon came to a small bridge with a little water running under it. I went under the bridge and sat on the grass by the side of the water. The realisation that the war was finally over hit me, and I wept for quite a few minutes. I thought, *why am I crying? It's good that there is no war. Millions of people must be rejoicing and celebrating.* But for me there was no reason to celebrate. I felt lost — I didn't know what would happen next. Would I evade the communists and join the Poles? If I did, I would never see my beloved country again and I felt very bitter. I had done everything I could to escape the terrible communist regime and I felt as if the whole world was against me. I also worried about my family. Now the communists were back in power, my family would again be evicted from our house. We should never have taken our Stepanivka house back, but how could we have known that? I felt homesick too. Would I ever be able to stop running from the communists?

* * *

I had to pull myself together and thought some food and a smoke

162

might help, so I opened the tin of corned beef, which had a small key attached to it, and used my small pocket knife to eat the meat and cut the bread. I then smoked two cigarettes and rested a while longer. I knew I had to get on with my life, so I got up and walked along the road until I reached the town I was headed for, Grottammare, on the coast of the Adriatic Sea.

As soon as I entered the town I saw two women in army uniform. They had "Poland" written on their sleeves too. I spoke to them in Ukrainian — they seemed to understand me but couldn't speak Ukrainian — and they spoke to each other in Polish. Then one of them opened her handbag and took out a twenty lire note — not an ordinary Italian note, but one used by the occupation forces. She turned it over and wrote something on it and told me to give it to the people at headquarters, pointing the way. I couldn't read what she had written on the note, but from the way she looked at me I was sure she had put a good word in for me. I was surprised that she looked at me in an interested sort of way — I must have looked absolutely terrible.

After a short walk I saw an officer, perhaps a captain, standing just inside the gate at the headquarters. He stood and stared at me, so I walked up to him and gave him the money with the writing on it. He read it and said to me in half-Polish, half-Ukrainian, 'So you want to join the Polish army?' I found out he could speak Ukrainian, Russian and Polish, so at last I managed to have a proper conversation with someone. He asked my name and I told him it was Stanislaw Wilsanski. I told him my parents had been Polish, even though I had lived in Ukraine all my life and couldn't speak Polish — exactly what Roman and I had planned I would say. Roman had told me that Ukrainians were accepted in the Polish division of the British army, but they would be more inclined to take me if they thought I was Polish.

While I lied about my background I told this Polish captain the truth about being forced to dig trenches for the German army. I also told him I didn't want to go back to the USSR. He took me to an office where three other officers interviewed me. They knew, as I did, that anyone who had worked for the German army would be shot. Even people who had been forced from their homes to work in Germany were given long prison sentences by the Soviets. The lucky ones found themselves in displaced persons camps in Germany after the war and a surprising amount of them managed to immigrate to countries such as America, Canada, Australia, Argentina, France, Belgium and Britain, especially if they had relatives in those countries. I don't know how they managed this, because the tiger hunters went everywhere looking for their victims. Perhaps they, like myself, lied about their nationalities.

I was fairly certain I would be safe with this Polish unit if they accepted me and believed my story. The Poles had no love for the Soviets and I reasoned that they were hardly likely to send me back if they thought I was Polish. But I was still very wary because, up until now, just about everyone I had met had tried to send me back to where I didn't want to go. One of the officers wrote down everything I said and told me that they would try to help me. Now that all my details were in writing, I would have to remember what I had told them — my life might depend on it. But I'd had plenty of time to rehearse my part since I said goodbye to Roman, so I felt sure that I would always be able to remember to tell the same story.

The first captain made a phone call and spoke for almost ten minutes. I couldn't understand what he said, but I couldn't help feeling that things would be better for me now, even though I was constantly on my guard. Then a jeep with a driver and unarmed corporal arrived and took me to a camp. They deposited me outside a barracks with a sign saying Barracks 8. I must have looked terrible — scratched, bruised and dirty, wearing very shabby civilian clothes, so it was no wonder that six young men stopped and stared at me. I spoke to them in Ukrainian and was quite surprised when I was answered in Ukrainian. The corporal took me to the main office where an officer asked me a few more questions, then I was taken to the quartermaster stores and given everything I would need to become a "Polish soldier" — British uniform, hat, underclothing, shoes, toilet articles and other gear. Carrying all this, I was taken to a long barrack room where ten other men were already billeted. They seemed friendly and talked to me for a few minutes, half in Polish and half in Ukrainian. I was shown to the showers and the corporal gave me a bag to put my dirty clothing in. He told me to remove any valuables from the pockets because the clothes would be thrown away. All I had of value was the Italian money I had started out with — not one Italian I had met would take money for helping me.

I was very dirty and it seemed ages since I'd had a proper wash. After I had dressed in my uniform, which was far too big for me, the corporal assigned two young men to show me around, asking them to tell me the Polish words for things as we went along, including the food and articles on the table. It was a typical army meal of meat and vegetables, and I was happy to be sitting at a table eating a substantial meal. I felt a bit safer now that I wasn't running. There were a lot of young Ukrainian men at this camp — they spoke Polish for general use and Ukrainian among themselves. They gave me a lot of help and told me how things were run. I asked why I hadn't been asked to sign any papers or been given a pay book, as in other armies. They said it all took time, but I thought the Polish authorities were probably trying to check up on me. But in the meantime I learned their way of drilling, exercising, the general rules and how to identify Polish ranks. Sometimes we would go for shooting practice in the hills, but my main job was working in the army motor workshop where they repaired lorries, jeeps, cars, motorbikes and our captain's old green Citroen car, which always needed something done to it. I knew almost nothing about motor vehicles, but because I had worked in a factory when I was younger, the others were prepared to help me and show me what needed to be done. I did the best I could.

* * *

In our spare time we would go to the beach and sometimes to cafes or a pub. But what we enjoyed most was the movies. Cowboy films were very popular even though they were in English, which nobody could understand. They weren't even subtitled, but we were still crazy for cowboy films. I liked the action and they were different to any film I had seen before. I would go in the afternoon when I had time off, and when that film had finished, I would go in the evening to another one at a different movie house.

I had been with the Poles for about two weeks when a messenger was sent to take me to the office. The messenger said there were strange officers waiting, as well as our own officers. I was afraid that they were Soviet officers come to get me, but they turned out to be Polish Military Intelligence personnel who had come to interview me more deeply. It was more like an interrogation as they tried to catch me out, making me repeat my story and parts of it over and over. I was scared, but soon realised from what they said that their objective was to find out if I was a spy working for the communists. I was very careful to stick to what I had said before, and by the end of the interview they decided I was all right. I had to sign a declaration to say I had told the truth and I was then allowed to sign a paper to join the Polish army. I was given an army pay book and had to swear an oath of allegiance to the British king and his family, and to the Polish government in exile.

A short while later the unit was moved to a town called San Bernadetto. We needed a larger base and a bigger workshop as more men were joining us. After only two weeks at San Bernadetto we moved again, this time to Senigallia. There were very good brick buildings at this base, which the Italian army had used before and during the war. The workshop was also very good and this is where I spent most of my time repairing motorbikes and jeeps. I had no real car driving experience, but I learnt to drive and would drive the jeeps around the huge yard.

Military police motorbikes would be brought in for checking and testing. If we felt like going for a spin in the country or up the mountain passes, we would put a notice on the back of the bikes saying "Testing", and take off for a really good day's riding. Once I rode with no goggles and not nearly enough clothing on, only a light battledress and trousers. I was soon very sorry — I could hardly see because of the wind and dust, and although it was a warm day, I found out how cold it could be riding a motorbike at speed. I felt chilled and not very well by the time I arrived back at the depot.

One day I was testing a motorbike in the yard of the depot and messing about a bit. I tried to turn around too quickly and I came half off, the heavy bike hitting my right leg. It was very painful and at first I thought that I had broken it. But I could stand on it all right and realised it couldn't be broken, although I carried a very large bruise for quite a while.

* * *

So far, throughout my life, I had had very little of what is thought of as the "good life", so now that I had a chance I began to live it up a bit. I smoked too many cigarettes and the cigarettes that I liked were very strong. As soon as I awoke in the morning, I would light a cigarette. Being in Italy, I also drank a lot of wine and other alcohol. Sometimes when we soldiers would have a meal in the cafes we would be served very poor wine, which I believe must have been diluted with something else. We would then be sick for a couple of days. There were a lot of very nice looking Italian girls who would give their favours for items such as chocolates, tinned beef, cigarettes or jars of jam. In a small town such as this they didn't have too many luxuries and sometimes were short of basic foods. But very soon I had found myself a steady girlfriend.

She was a young widow named Gina and she had two small children, a boy aged four and a girl of about two. They lived across the road from the workshop where I worked. When it was nearly time for me to finish work she would come to her window and signal to me to hurry up. She was a very lovely woman with long black hair and a good figure, and she dressed very nicely. She had known some of the other men, but now that we were courting we kept ourselves for each other. She was twenty-two and I was twenty-three. She was a very special person to me and I may have married her if I had stayed in Italy. I would take her any gifts that I could, especially food. We were good friends as well as lovers and I had learnt quite a bit of the Italian language so we talked a lot. She told me that although she was looked upon as a widow, she wasn't sure her husband was dead. He had been a captain in the Italian army and sent to the Eastern front, from where he had not returned. I believe she and her family had been quite affluent before the war. Her flat was large, airy and clean, with a very good kitchen, good furniture, nice paintings on the walls and bric-a-brac scattered through the rooms.

Every Saturday there was a large outdoor market near the church. Even though we didn't need anything, we soldiers would go just for a look around. It was very interesting and I noticed that very good quality items were sold there. I guessed they were objects that people had owned before the war and now had to sell because of reduced circumstances. One day I was shopping in town and stopped to look in a shop window. I was trying to decide whether to go in when a young monk came and stood very close to me, holding a bicycle pump and pushing it in and out. I looked to see what he was doing and he suddenly pushed the pump into my private parts. I thought at first it must have been an accident, but when I looked at him he gave me a sort of sheepish smile. I was shocked and moved away quickly. Until then I had thought churchmen were holy and didn't do those sorts of things.

The seaside wasn't far away and sometimes we would sit in the sun or just walk along the beach. Once a few of us found an abandoned Italian two-man submarine, half-buried in the sand. We would also swim, which I enjoyed as I was a reasonably good swimmer. I also liked to go out in the rowing boats. One day I was rowing and I think the rowing motion must have unscrewed my divisional badge because I lost it and never found it again. I was very sorry about this — they would only issue one to each man and I couldn't get another. I had hoped that I might be able to keep it as a souvenir when I was discharged at some future date.

The army depot was not far from the railway station and one day we saw a group of men walking into the station with red flags displaying the dreaded hammer and sickle, and also placards and posters. They were obviously going to meet a train, so not wanting to get involved, we stood at a safe distance and watched. As the train, heavily crowded with men, arrived at the platform the waiting people, obviously communists, surged forward to greet the incoming passengers, waving the flags and shouting, 'Viva Russia!' and 'Viva Stalin!'. As soon as the train trundled to a halt, the men on board rushed onto the platform like a stampeding herd of very angry buffalo and attacked the waiting communists, tearing the flags to shreds. It was like a riot. The Italian police came and broke it up, ordering the men from the train back on board and sending the train further along the line. We were close enough to see everything without being in trouble's way and when it was all over, we walked back to our depot. When we mentioned the incident we were told that the men on the train had been prisoners in the Soviet Union who had been freed and were now returning home. Having been prisoners of the Soviet Union they knew exactly what communism was really like.

I was now supposed to be a Roman Catholic, so when Christmas 1945 arrived I celebrated on December 25th, not January 7th as I had done all my life. I had a meal with some other Ukrainians who must have guessed I was really Ukrainian, although nothing was said, then I took presents to Gina and the children. I realised that my own Christmas, which would have been at the beginning of 1945, had been lost. I just couldn't remember where I had been at the time, but I wasn't surprised — it hadn't been the sort of time when you could think of things like Christmas. On New Year's Eve 1945 to New Year's Day 1946, I celebrated with everyone else on December 31st and January 1st. We could hear some of the Italians singing communist songs, so we Ukrainians and Poles shot our machine guns and rifles into the air thinking we might scare them. Up till midnight we all got quite drunk, then once we had seen the New Year in, we fell asleep. We still had to get up later in the morning and go to work as usual.

I had become quite friendly with a Polish man called Wilhem Zabinski. I called him Willy. He came from the Western part of Poland, very close to the German and Czechoslovakian border, and was about five years older than me. We used to drink a lot together and he suggested that I go with him back home. Of course, he thought I was Polish but he knew that I was afraid to go back to that part of the world. He told me that his family had a picture house; he was the manager and he offered me a job. He said he really would like me to go back with him and meet his wife and two children, but I was scared stiff to go anywhere in Eastern Europe. I knew the Soviets had already occupied the eastern part of Poland and when I mentioned it he said, 'Don't worry about that, they won't harm you. I will protect you.' I realised he really had no idea what communism was like. I declined his offer.

Willy and I were out one night and had already had a few too many drinks when somehow he got into a fight with three Italians. I rushed over to help him — I can't remember much about it, but it seems I gave one of the Italians three pricks with the part of my pocketknife that was supposed to be used for taking stones out of horses' hooves. I must have been very drunk as I don't like knives at all and a small utility knife is all I ever carried. The Italians left and we walked — or maybe staggered — back to the depot. The next day we were called to the main office. The Italians had come to complain. They were all right, the pricks I had given the Italian hadn't even punctured the skin. I couldn't remember much about the incident, but we both apologised to them and our commanding officer told us, in front of the Italians, that we were both sentenced to three days in the army jail.

This so-called prison was a dim cellar. We had clean mattresses to sleep on and good food brought down to us. Most of the time we just sat and talked and we had visitors who brought us wine. We were allowed to come out each day for exercise. It was supposed to be punishment, but after the rough way I had lived it was like a luxury hotel. The general idea was to placate the Italians and show that justice had been carried out. After three days we both went back to work.

I was still courting Gina and life was going along in a normal way when, about a month after the incident with the Italians, we were told that if anyone wanted to go back to Poland they could. Willy decided to go. He had always intended to do so and asked me once again to go with him. I refused, so we wished each other good luck and soon after he and six other men left the base. I never saw Willy again.

CHAPTER XV

The brink of death

For about a year everything went on normally. I was still visiting Gina and doing my usual work, but I began to feel very unwell. I had always been a strong person but now I was short of breath, coughing all the time feeling very weak. Then I noticed I was coughing up brown phlegm. I decided something was really wrong. I knew I hadn't been looking after myself properly and suspected that my time as a trench digger had also done me no good.

I stopped smoking because it made me feel worse. When the boys in the workshop heard this they said, 'Oh come on, smoking never hurt anyone, have a cigarette', so someone lit one and gave it to me. It made me so sick that I decided that was the last cigarette I would ever smoke. Instead I walked around with a packet of boiled sweets in my pocket and would suck one if I felt the urge to smoke. I wasn't getting any better so I visited the army doctor who, after examining me, rang for a jeep to take me to the hospital for an X-ray. He also rang my commanding officer.

The hospital was only two kilometres away. I was taken for an X-ray straight away and half an hour later one of the doctors told me that I had inflammation of the left lung. He said he would ring for transport so that I could go back to my billet and collect my belongings. I would then have to come back and be admitted to the hospital immediately. When I arrived back at my billet I dropped in to see my mates at the workshop. When I told them I had inflammation of the lung, they were very sorry as they believed it to be a serious illness. I had no idea how sick I was. I thought it didn't sound too serious and hoped they were wrong.

After I had put my belongings in the jeep, the driver waited for me while I went over the road to say goodbye to Gina. She was very sorry to hear I was sick and asked how long I would be in hospital. I told her I didn't know. She wished me good luck and gave me a kiss. She was sure I wouldn't be away long. That was the last time I ever saw Gina. There was no way I could know if she tried to see me. I was admitted to the infectious diseases area which nobody was allowed to visit.

* * *

I was shown to a large ward where there were six beds. Five of them were already occupied and I took the last vacant one, which was in the middle of the room. I soon found out we all had the same illness, even though I still didn't know what it was called. We all talked a lot, got to know each other and became mates. Four of the men were Polish and one was Russian. I was the only Ukrainian in the ward, but they didn't know that. The sister who was assigned to our room was a friendly woman about twenty-five years old who was also very attractive, even though she had a large, very noticeable scar on her face near her mouth. We all liked her and she looked after us very well. I found out later that she was Ukrainian.

A few weeks after I entered hospital, I suddenly awoke one night feeling as if I was choking. I couldn't breathe and I was very frightened. I sat up, made a choking sort of cough and blood gushed from my mouth and nose. It went absolutely everywhere. Everyone else woke up and the sister, who must have been very close at hand, switched on the light and hurried over to me. She put a towel on my chest to catch the blood, but it soaked the sheets, blankets and floor. She told me to keep calm and stay still, then ran out of the room, racing back with two bags of ice which she put on my chest and head. I realised later that she had saved my life. She knew just what to do and I have always been very grateful to her. She propped me up with pillows and told me I would have to sit up in bed all night. The ice helped stem the flow of blood and slowly, over the next half hour, the flow lessened and then stopped, but twice when I coughed I brought up quite a lot of blood. The sister was doing other duties but looked in from time to time to see how I was. Once the blood had stopped she changed the top sheets, blankets and towels and cleaned up as much as she could without moving me. She brought me a hospital bottle to use as a toilet. Then she told the other men to go back to sleep and turned the light off.

I had to sit up all night and I could see that she had left the door into the corridor open and the passage light on. It was a comfort to be able to see that light and know that she wouldn't be very far away if I needed help. She came in every fifteen minutes or so to check on me. After a while I started to feel a little better, but blood was still coming up when I coughed. I used a towel the sister had brought me and a little later she brought lots of paper towels. I didn't get much sleep that night.

When the sister was out of the room and the other men were sleeping I began to pray silently. I couldn't have spoken if I had wanted to. 'God, I want to live. I've tried so hard to stay alive and look for a better life. I'm only twenty-four, surely I'm too young to leave this world yet. I will put up with any treatment and live a healthier life.' I prayed very hard, asking repeatedly for help to become healthy. I'd had reason to pray for help before, but never with as much hope, faith and meaning as I did then.

For the next few days I continued to lose blood and had to sit still with pillows behind me. They started bringing me soft food and warm milk and I managed to make myself eat and drink. In the days that followed, the staff asked me what I would like to eat. I often fancied warm milk and sometimes for the midday meal I would have mashed potatoes and mashed fish or a small amount of finely chopped meat and vegetable. But there were times when I had no appetite at all. Although I was allowed to eat and drink I was told that I must not speak at all as it caused vibrations in the lungs, which could be very dangerous for me. So I made hand signs or pointed to the menu instead.

We were given no medical treatment in this hospital, only bed rest and good food. I stayed about five weeks then, along with four others, was taken by military ambulance to a hospital in the town of San Loretto, famous for its very ancient church and for its spectacular scenery. The hospital was on a hillside and I think the medical authorities believed that the cooler air would be good for patients suffering from tuberculosis. I knew that this was the correct name for the disease, which my companions and I had contracted.

Again we had no medical treatment, only good food and rest. I believe that they did not have any treatment for tuberculosis in Italy at the time. I was still weak, but I was starting to slowly move about. I could not go very far but walked in the very attractive garden of the hospital. I would also stand on the hospital balcony and look at the very picturesque countryside and the huge old church. I still have postcards of San Loretto and the church, which I bought at the hospital shop, and a photograph of myself with five other men taken on the hospital balcony.

I was at that hospital for just over three weeks because the entire Polish section of the British army was to be transferred to Britain. The Polish medical staff started selling everything to the Italians — cars, ambulances, beds, medical equipment and bedding. I suppose they had been told not to bring much to Britain.

We sick men were put on stretchers and taken by ambulance to a train bound for Naples. My stretcher was loaded on to the top shelf in one of the carriages. There were many other sick people already on board and also a staff of doctors, sisters and nurses. I don't know who the people in my carriage were, but it was hell for me because it was very hot and most of them were smoking. All the heat and smoke rose up to engulf me and made me feel absolutely terrible — as if every breath would be my last. I was very weak, but I tried to get to the floor and when the others saw that I wanted to get down they helped me. There was not enough room for me to lay down but I managed to stand and then sit on the floor. It was cooler and not as polluted as up near the roof. When we reached Naples, the train went right up to the docks where a ship was waiting. Someone took my stretcher down so I could lie on it, and then I was taken from the train and put on the grass while we waited to be loaded onto the ship.

The weather was very warm but I could still feel the damp grass, even though the stretcher had small legs on it. A couple of dozen people lay on stretchers while the paper work was checked. I was wearing pyjamas and a light dressing gown and socks. I had a small suitcase under my head containing a few odds and ends such as photos, postcards, a few coins and notes, my pay book, hankies, socks and toilet articles. That was all I had to take with me to Britain. Some people came around checking our names. When they came to check my name, they looked down at me and I heard someone say in Polish, 'Why are you taking these more than half-dead people with you? Why not leave them here to die? This one won't last a couple of weeks.' A woman's voice answered, 'Give them a chance, let them go on the ship.'

BOOK III

Survival

CHAPTER XVI

Safe at last

I TRULY believe that if I had been left in San Loretto I would have died. Apart from not having any medicine for my condition, the weather had become very hot and heavy. Once we had been loaded onto the ship, I was taken to a very large cabin which had been made into a ward with ten hospital-style beds, surrounded by rails to prevent the patients falling out. My bed was near the porthole. As the ship started out to sea I was surprised how quickly I began to feel better. It was almost immediate — the cool sea air was so refreshing after the humid climate of Italy.

It took about a week to cross the Mediterranean Sea and the medical staff looked after us very well. We had to stay in bed for the first few days, but soon everyone was feeling much better and was able to eat more, gradually gaining the strength to get out of bed and move about. Those who could manage it would go to the canteen for meals. I felt so much better; like a different person. The sea air suited me, and although I was still coughing a lot I really wanted to get better, so I tried to walk to the canteen for as many meals as I could.

Sometimes I would sit in bed and read; I also tried to walk on the deck to feel the breeze and look at the sea — something I have always liked to do. The weather was very good for most of our voyage, but it became rough around the Bay of Biscay, which is normal for that area. Of course, we sick people stayed in our beds when the weather was rough. As we approached the shores of Britain the weather became cooler and cooler, but this seemed to help the patients with lung problems.

We docked at Southampton and were taken on stretchers to a waiting train which took us to Witchurch, in Shropshire. We were then taken six miles by ambulance to a very large, old hospital at a place called Iscote Park. This old barrack-style hospital was being used by the Polish authorities as a tuberculosis hospital. It was now the winter of 1947 and it was very cold. The whole countryside was covered with very thick snow. There were other large barrack-type buildings near the hospital and I thought the whole place must have once been used by the British army as military barracks.

The ward I was assigned to was very large and contained forty beds, twenty down each side. The ward was heated by two black coke-burning stoves, with long pipe-like chimneys going up and out through the roof. The coke made some fumes and we were told we could open the windows if it bothered us. The floor was made of asphalt on concrete and was black and shiny. Although the stoves gave a reasonable amount of heat, the ward was cold most of the time. We had a woman doctor looking after us. She was a specialist in the treatment of tuberculosis. She was a Tartar, which means she must have been a descendant of the Mongolian Golden Horde of Ghengis Khan. She was small, friendly, cheerful and efficient and often joked with us. Another patient in my ward, Basil, really fancied this doctor whose name, Murrza Murzich, was a name and title meaning "lady" or "nobility" in her language. I liked her, but not in the way Basil did — she was a bit old for me. I liked looking at the younger nurses and sisters. Basil and I became very friendly during our time in the ward together; we got on very well, like brothers. In fact he looked a lot like I thought my brother Michael, who I believed had been killed by the communists, would look now.

Every morning the nurses would come around the ward taking samples of our phlegm on a glass slide to find out how much *tubercular bacilli* was in our lungs. I was told I would soon have treatment and on the day my treatment started I was taken to a clinic where about twenty-five other men were waiting. When my turn came, I stood stripped to the waist in front of a screen while the doctor took X-ray pictures. Then she told me she was going to put air in my left lung, between the lung and the rib cage, so that the lung could not expand too far, allowing it to rest and heal more quickly. I had to lie on a table on my right side and put my left arm up. A sister helped but the doctor did most of the work. She pressed my ribs to separate them and this tickled me and made me laugh and move. She told me to relax and not move at all — it could be very dangerous if the needle bent or broke. It was a large needle as it had to pump air into the body. The procedure was very painful but I bore it with no complaint as I was pleased to be receiving some treatment.

* * *

Each day I was silently thanking God for each step of progress I made. I was determined to recover from the tuberculosis even though at times I had thought I would die. Once a week, mostly Wednesdays, I would have an X-ray and the needle treatment. Patients wore pyjamas, dressing gowns, socks and slippers most of the time, and after a while we were given loose navy blue trousers and jackets, which we could wear over our bed clothing. We were also given some shoes so that when the weather allowed, we could walk outside in a small wood which at certain times of the year was carpeted by thousands of bluebells. It was a beautiful little wood, with a small stream running through it. Sometimes we would walk along the path beside a sealed road and soon I was walking up to five miles a day to help get my strength back. There were a lot of stately old homes in the area and the local people knew the men walking around were from the hospital.

The army still paid us wages while we were in hospital, so I bought extra food for myself. I liked salted herrings, which were not very salty in Britain, but they helped my appetite. Someone told me cod liver oil contained good vitamins, so I bought a bottle and forced myself to swallow some of it every day. I bought grapes, which were expensive, and a variety of different foods so that I had a change from the hospital fare. I started to feel a lot better and I could see that some of the other men in our ward were making good progress too. But it was terrible to see men I had become friendly with going downhill. In our large ward, some men became so ill they had to be given oxygen masks. Often someone would die in the night and be gone when we woke in the morning. I believe that the hospital staff experimented on the men, but I am sure they meant it for the best.

Quite a few would be taken to the operating theatre and while under anaesthetic, their ribs on one side of their back would be cut right through and pushed on to the lung, so that the patient could not use that lung. Their backs were caved in and special jackets were made for them so that they would look normal when outside the hospital. Although most of these men didn't die, they were permanent invalids.

* * *

My good friend Basil was a very clever person and liked to play chess. He was quite a champion at the game. He offered to teach me but I said that I couldn't manage that sort of game and was too impatient. He jokingly said he would like to have all the brains I was short of. It was our special joke. We would go out walking together and sit together reading Ukrainian and Polish books borrowed from the hospital library. I also sent away for Ukrainian books and newspapers from the Ukrainian Association of Great Britain, in London, and I borrowed books from other Ukrainians. Because he was Ukrainian we had no secrets from each other, so I told him my story. He was twenty-four and I was twenty-six.

One day a doctor told Basil about a new drug called strep-tomycin, which had been used with a degree of success against tuberculosis, but which was also very expensive. Basil, who had slowly been getting better, had saved some money and decided to try the new treatment, which cost 300 English pounds — an enormous amount of money in those days. He received ten injec-tions over a period of time and we thought the medicine was working as he seemed much better. But Basil had a sudden relapse and deteriorated very quickly. The staff put him in a private room and gave him an oxygen mask. I would go in and talk to him and read books or newspapers sometimes late into the night. I also brought him food. He would take his mask off and try to eat. I used to bring him grapes and other luxury food and he would try to eat to please me. The hospital allowed patients to use some small kitchens, so I cooked chicken for him one day and soup another time. I would shop for him, and he asked me to talk to our doctor about getting another course of streptomycin, hoping it would help him get better. He still had enough money, so the staff allowed him to try a second course of ten injections. How-ever, he became worse.

Basil knew he would probably die, so he decided to make a will. A lawyer was brought in and the doctors served as witnesses. Just over a week later, at about seven am, a sister came to tell me Basil had died in the night. Two hours later I was allowed to go to the mortuary to see him and say goodbye. While I was down there, six other Ukrainians came down to also say goodbye to his spirit. His body was already in a coffin. One of the Ukrainians had a camera and took photos of Basil in his coffin to send to his family in Ukraine, so that they would be absolutely sure what had happened to him. A week later, when the photos came back from being developed, we composed a letter, which we found to be a difficult task, and enclosed the photos. His parents wrote back and thanked us for our kind words and for letting them know what had happened to him. On the second day after Basil's death, a Polish service was held for him in the hospital chapel. He was buried in the cemetery in the small village of Iscote Park. We Ukrainians knew he was a Ukrainian, but like myself and some of the others he had been posing as a Pole. Even though he was Greek Catholic rather than Roman Catholic we, his friends, felt that he had been given the right type of religious service.

* * *

I really missed Basil; he had been like a younger brother to me. I had seen so very little of my own brother, Michael, except when we were very young. Three days after the funeral, Basil's will was read and I discovered he had left all his belongings to me — a wrist watch, a small radio, some photographs, his army belt, some pound notes and the emblem from the cap he wore when he, like others, had been forced into the German army. There was also a bayonet. Sometime later someone stole the watch and the bayonet had to be handed in. I used the radio for a long time but the only things I have now are the belt and photos. I'm not sure what happened to the badge but I still have good memories of my friend Basil.

I had known Basil for only just over a year, but his death hit me very hard. I had thought that at last I had found a friend who I would not have to leave, but as fate would have it he had to leave me and the other friends he had made. I had lived a lot of my life on my own and it had been good to have a friend. Although I came from a big family, because of circumstances I had spent very little time with them. I and others had done everything we could to keep Basil alive but his body was too weak and there was very little treatment for tuberculosis in those days and the new drug may not have suited him.

* * *

Life at the hospital carried on, although we all felt the absence of Basil. One day the hospital dentist came round to check our teeth. When he checked mine he told me I had beautiful teeth, perfectly formed and first class colour. He offered me fifty pounds on the spot if I would leave my teeth to him in my will. The sum of fifty pounds was a lot of money in those days and his offer frightened me. He must have thought I was going to die — but I had decided I was definitely going to live. I had wild thoughts like, *what if he kills me or takes my teeth while I am still alive?* I knew this was silly, but he did scare me, so I said no. Now that I think of it, if I had taken the money he would have had to wait a long time and come a long way to collect them. They are not quite as good now.

* * *

The countryside around Iscote Park was very beautiful and very peaceful. There was very little traffic, even on the main road. Every day any staff who were not on duty, and any patients who were well enough, would go for long walks and on one such day we came across a gypsy encampment in a small field near the side of the road. They stayed for about a week and we saw them every day as we passed by. They were real gypsies not tinkers. The women wore fancy embroidered blouses with lots of beads, large earrings and long skirts. The men were dressed as you would expect gypsies to be and they also wore earrings, only smaller ones. There were six vehicles; two old buses and four lovely caravans drawn by horses. These were real gypsy-style wooden houses on wheels and were covered with paintings of flowers and other colourful designs. They had pipe chimneys through the roof. We guessed that these were for cooking and heating inside as gypsies in Britain can't spend as much time outdoors as they do in other countries because of the inclement weather.

I was still progressing well and after a while my treatment was changed. The needle with air was now put in my stomach to squash the lung, and I received this treatment twice a week. It did seem to help, and after three months of this I was given a small operation on the left side of my neck. I believe they did something to a nerve going to the lung. They explained what treatment they had given me but I didn't really understand what was said. I knew, however, that everything possible was being done to help all of us. I continued to have the air treatment twice a week for just over six months. It was quite an ordeal, but I felt I was getting better and I made sure I never complained. I also kept trying to help myself by buying extra food, cod liver oil and orange juice at the hospital shop and I tried to exercise by walking as far as I could as often as possible.

From the time I first arrived at Iscote Park I had spent about one year in this hospital. Although my new treatment finished after six months, I was kept in hospital for rest and recuperation. It was at about this time that the Polish units of the British army were disbanded and the soldiers demobilised. The British government tried to persuade as many Poles as possible to return to Poland, mostly by advertising in the Polish newspapers. For those who really didn't want to go back, a new organisation was

formed called the Polish Resettlement Corps or PRC. Polish
soldiers were encouraged to find civilian jobs outside the camps.
Until we could be resettled we were still paid normal army wages.
Since I had been with the Poles I had been shocked to find out
how much some of them hated Ukrainians. They thought I was
Polish so I heard and read things that I wouldn't ordinarily have
known about.

* * *

At last I began to feel really well, although I still had X-rays every
week. When the hospital staff saw how well I was doing, they
decided I could leave hospital and go to a convalescent camp in
Berkshire. I and a few other men were taken by car to the railway
station, then the train took us to a camp which was near Newbury,
but I can't remember its name. It must have been a British army
base before being used as a convalescent camp. Each room had
about twenty beds, ten down each side, and was very long and
barrack-like. It looked very much like a hospital, but we did have
more room for our possessions than in hospital. Some of the men
had pushbikes, which they left in the corridors. I didn't have one
but the men would lend me theirs when they were not using them
and I would go for long rides outside the camp, sometimes alone,
but more often with some of the other men.

We were still under the overall control of the British army, but
the camp was run by the Polish authorities. The Polish are very
religious people and our commandant was even more so. He also
liked to please the priest, so every morning and every evening
at lights out the religious song *Ave Maria* was played over the
loud speakers. We had to listen to it if we wanted to or not. It is a
very nice song, but not all the time. I got absolutely fed up with
hearing it.

I went for walks in a lovely forest outside the camp where I would gather chestnuts and hazelnuts. I didn't know if it was a private forest but nobody told me so, and nobody stopped me walking there. The year was 1948. One day I was walking in the forest when I found a horseshoe. I didn't need it, so I threw it away. When I arrived back at my barrack, I picked up my battle dress jacket from the back of the chair where I had draped it and found that someone had stolen my wallet. It only had a few pounds in it, but I was upset that my pay book was also gone. I treasured it as it was a reminder of the time in 1945 when I had been issued with it and allowed to join the British army; a turning point in my life, when I had stopped running away from the communists. I thought, *this bad luck has come to me because I threw that horseshoe away.* The next day I went back to the forest and looked everywhere for it, retracing my steps. I was so sure that I knew exactly where I had thrown it. But look as I may — and I spent a long time looking — I just could not find it. I reported the theft to the commandant and the military police, and I was issued with a new book.

* * *

When the weather was good enough I would sit outside the barracks with some of the other men and we would talk. Mostly I would listen, and it was then that I realised how much some Poles hated Ukrainians. They all thought I was Polish, so I found out things I normally would never have known. Most of the western part of Ukraine had been occupied by Poland and some of the older men said they were colonists, who had been given Ukrainian land after World War I and had built on it. They boasted about how they had desecrated some of the Ukrainian Orthodox churches by rubbing human waste, oil, tar and other rubbish on the altars, smashing the icons and other religious artifacts. They said their government had produced a booklet on how to harass and annoy the Ukrainians as much as possible. They were told that if they knew any of the Ukrainian language they must not use it and only speak Polish or Russian to the Ukrainians. Some Ukrainians are Catholics, but follow Greek Catholicism. Ukrainians who would change their religion and become Roman Catholics would be treated better, given some privileges and in some cases allowed to own land. I discovered that Poles have always had this dream called Big Poland sea to sea, which means they would like to occupy all the land from the Baltic Sea to the Black Sea, which included a lot of Ukrainian territory. They had been angry for centuries because in the very olden times, the Ukrainian Zaparishian Cossacks threw them out of many parts of Ukraine. Although after that the Russians occupied much of Ukraine, for most of known history Ukraine has been occupied, mostly by either Poland or Russia, as well as more recently by the Germans and other races further back in history.

This was the first time I had heard many of these things, coming as I do from the Russian occupied areas. I had taught myself to read Polish from newspapers so I decided to find out more and borrowed some books from the library, I borrowed three books which made up a trilogy called *By Fire and Sword*. I was horrified by what I read. The books told of how the Poles had treated the Ukrainians throughout the ages. They told of a time the Poles captured some Cossacks and tied them in such a way that they were able to slice off three heads with one stroke of a sword, an achievement I find hard to believe. They also described horrible torture the Poles had performed on Ukrainians. These are so terrible I feel I cannot explain them here as I hope young people might read my story. I stopped reading the books and put them away, ready to take back to the library. But after a few days

I decided that I must know what was in them and how the Poles thought and felt.

It seems, according to the men in the hospital and some of the books I read, that before World War II, the Poles rounded up hundreds of Ukrainian intellectuals and known nationalists and took them on a forced march in very hot and dusty conditions to a notorious concentration camp called Bereza-Katuska. The Soviets and Germans did the same type of thing to the Ukrainians when they were in power. I don't want the reader to think that I found all the Polish people like this, but the ones who had lived in the western part of Ukraine were. I have had many good friends who are Polish, but they were from the western part of Poland. I along with other Ukrainians have often thought that it would have been a good thing if Ukraine and Poland could have been better friends. Together they might have had more chance against communism and the Soviets. But unfortunately some Poles would work with Satan himself if it would hurt the Ukrainians.

* * *

Towards the end of 1948 and early in 1949, we were all being slowly demobilised from the British army and I thought it was about time I had a civilian suit. At that time in Britain, many things were still rationed and people needed coupons as well as money to buy clothes. The army was still providing our clothing needs so I had no clothing coupons, but when one Polish man from the next block of barracks told me he was going to London for the day to do some shopping, I said I would go with him. He said he knew his way around one area and he would take me to a small shop where I could get a good suit without coupons. So we travelled to London by train and then to the centre of one of the city's shopping areas. I didn't like travelling in the London underground, it had a feeling of being very old, very deep and very badly ventilated. I found the air very heavy and hard to breathe. It wasn't a patch on the metro I had seen when travelling through Moscow. When we arrived at the shopping centre near Hyde Park, this Polish man, whose name I can't recall, took me down some steps to a small cellar-like clothing shop.

My companion spoke in English to the Jewish proprietor of the shop. He did all the talking because my command of the English language was very poor. I was told that the shopkeeper said, 'Don't worry about coupons, I'm sure I can find something which will suit you.' He measured me, then brought out a dark bluish-grey suit, which looked very nice. I tried it on and it fitted me well. It looked very good and I was pleased as this was the first time I had ever had a suit. It cost fourteen pounds which was an awful lot of money in those days — a full month's wage — but I liked it and thought if I looked after it, it would last for years. The shopkeeper wrapped it in brown paper and tied string around it. I paid and we left the shop. We looked at a few other shops and bought a few small things, then travelled back to the camp by train.

When we got back I couldn't wait to show off my new suit to some of the other men in our barracks. When I tried it on, one old Ukrainian chap I only knew by the name Zaychuck said, 'You're crazy, you should never have paid fourteen pounds for such rubbish, take it back.' Then he showed me how it was falling to pieces, especially on the inside legs. He suggested that the poor sewing meant that the suit had been made to fit a corpse to wear in its coffin and he kept insisting that I take it back, saying I had been robbed. I was shocked and very disappointed. I was sure the suit in the shop was perfect because I had examined it closely and admired it because I had never before had a suit. I came to the conclusion that the suit had been switched before I picked it up.

I decided to take it back but I didn't know where the shop was and when I asked the Polish chap who had taken me there he flatly refused to take me or even give me directions. I believe he must have also been in on the scam. You can imagine how very disappointed I was. This was my very first suit and I've never forgotten what a letdown it was. I had to wear it, which meant I had to keep sewing it up. I decided to save up for another suit and wait until coupons were no longer needed. It was almost two years before I bought another suit and by that time I had moved away from this camp.

* * *

Soon after this, about twenty-four of us were moved to another camp near Southampton, very close to the town of Havant. I started going around with a few casual girlfriends, but I got fed up with this and longed for a proper relationship with a nice girl. The weather was very cold and I caught the flu. Because I had just recovered from TB the camp authorities were afraid I might have contracted it again so they sent me back to the hospital at Iscote Park. I didn't get my old barrack back, but they all looked the same. They X-rayed me and did many tests. They found that the tuberculosis had flared up again and although it wasn't very bad I would have to stay there for quite a while. Now that I was back in hospital and it looked like a long stay, I was issued with hospital clothing.

This time the only treatment I received was rest and moderate exercise under supervision. They kept a check on my condition by taking samples of phlegm each morning. I was given X-rays once a week and then later once or twice a month. I bought extra food for myself and cod liver oil which I took each day. We were given fresh orange juice each day and I drank raw eggs with wine and sugar. I also bought salted herrings, salami and pickled gherkins, which gave me an appetite, and other food including fruit, which I was told was good for me. After six months they told me I was clear and had no tuberculosis bacilli in my body. They told me that although they were pleased with the result, because I had suffered a relapse I must stay in the hospital a while longer so they could monitor my condition.

* * *

Not long after, I had been given a clean bill of health, a man I had never seen before was shown around and given a bed which was three beds away from mine. I noticed he had a lot of Ukrainian books and magazines with him. I went over to him and said, 'Hello, you're Ukrainian, are you?' He told me he was and said he came from Kiev, our capital city. He told me his name was Inas Omilianenko and I found that he was a very well-educated man. He was also a great talker and very interesting. We became quite friendly and would often walk together in the wood. He had an air pistol and we would shoot at bottles and cans. It was like a toy, even though the lead pellets could have been dangerous. We were very careful and enjoyed playing with it.

He told me he had been working in London and had developed a persistent cough. He had gone for an X-ray and a dark spot had been found on one of his lungs, so he had been sent to this hospital. Luckily they found that he was not very sick and he only stayed at the hospital about two months. He said he had not been in any of the services but was a displaced civilian who had come from Germany. When he arrived in Britain he had to sign a contract stating that for two years he would work at any job and go anywhere the authorities sent him. When he arrived at the hospital he had already done this and was a free man.

He could speak, read and write English and had a pen-pal in America. I don't know if he had other pen-pals or not. His friend was a middle-aged woman. He must have mentioned me in his letters to her. She started to put letters in for me with Inas' letters and he would read them to me and write back to her on my behalf. She seemed a very nice person and told me about her life and family. In one letter she said she was recovering from a nervous breakdown. I wondered how she had come to suffer a breakdown. Her life seemed so normal, even luxurious.

When Inas left he continued to write to her, but let her know that my English wasn't good enough for me to continue corresponding with her. Inas told me he belonged to the Ukrainian Nationalist Organisation and told me quite a lot about it. I couldn't join because they needed educated people who could help their work, but I was very interested in them and he copied their oath and some of their programs for me. He also gave me some of their literature. Although I wasn't in the organisation I believed in and supported what they stood for. They were very patriotic, as I considered myself to be.

Twice, Inas and I travelled to London by train. We really went to look around, but we also did a little shopping. We stayed overnight both times at the Ukrainian Association in Great Britain, which was affiliated with the Ukrainian Nationalist Organisation of which Inas was a member. They had rooms with four beds each. We were shown to a room already occupied by two men. We had a look around the club, which had a library, kitchen, canteen and printing machine office. When we were sitting in the canteen the first time we visited, Inas whispered to me to draw my attention to a very elderly man who must have been in his late eighties, saying, 'That is Vadim Shcerbakivski.' Inas was very impressed by this man, who he said was a very famous person — a scientist, archaeologist, professor and highly intellectual. I had never heard of him. I just felt sorry for the old man who looked so very old and rather sick. Later I read about him and I was also quite impressed. He had done many things and was one of the archaeologists who had explored the famous rock grave. Inas told me about other famous Ukrainians who were there, but I had never heard of them either, not having moved in those circles. But I could have been interested in many things he talked about if we had been together for a longer time.

He left hospital after two months and, even though I'd only known him a short time, I missed him. He said he would keep in touch and later wrote and told me he had travelled up to London, finding a job on the outskirts of the city in a factory. He was also going to night school to learn to repair clocks and watches. He was already a writer and journalist.

CHAPTER XVII

Kathleen

A FTER Inas departed, I started going out alone and decided to have a look at some of the nearest large cities and towns. I was feeling very well and it was the first time in my life that I had been healthy and not working. I was still in the army so received a small wage but my uniform was put away and when I went out I dressed in civilian clothes; not in *that* suit, but a jacket and trousers. I had to ask permission to leave the hospital and I spoke to Doctor Murrza-Murzich, who arranged a few days leave for me. I was glad to have a short holiday away from the hospital.

I heard from other Ukrainians that there was going to be a big Ukrainian rally and concert in Manchester, so I travelled by train as far as Crewe where I had to change trains. It was a warm day and I noticed the sun looked quite big as I boarded the train for Manchester. However, when I arrived in Manchester, which is only a short distance from Crewe, I found the city so polluted that I could only see a small pinprick of the sun shining through the smog. I rented a room for two days. It was a bed and breakfast place and cost twelve shillings and sixpence a day, which was reasonable. It must have been a family concern as the mother did the cooking and managed the place, while her daughter acted as waitress and also cleaned up and made the beds. The breakfasts were quite good. I was served eggs, beans, toast with marmalade and tea on both days.

There were not many guests and I was given a room with two beds. In the morning I looked around the shops and did some window shopping. In the afternoon I went to the rally. Many Ukrainians, some in national costume, walked along the streets with banners and flags and I walked with them. We came to a stadium with an open air stage, very much like the Myer Music Bowl in Melbourne. There were speeches, poems and some singing, mostly political. After the rally I attended the concert. The performers wore national dress and the performances included singing, dancing and speeches. They spoke up against communism, the Russians and the Soviet regime in general. I was surprised and pleased that we were allowed to hold rallies, concerts and to speak freely in Britain. I really enjoyed the whole day and took photos of both the rally and concert.

The next morning, before I went out, the pretty young daughter of the house came to my room while I was still there to clean the vanity unit and make the bed. She was very friendly and I thought how pretty she was. I came very close to her and she didn't push me away. We started playing around, pretending to chase each other. After a short time she allowed me to make love to her. The only thing she was worried about was making sure the door was locked so that her mother would not know.

* * *

I didn't like Manchester; it was so dirty and polluted. I walked around sightseeing on the second day and after two hours my hands and face were black with grime. Manchester, Liverpool and Birkenhead are not very far apart so I decided to visit them all. Liverpool seemed to me to be poor and dirty, as you might expect of a large port. I mostly window-shopped there. Everywhere I visited in the city seemed to be crowded with sailors from all parts of the world; there were very many ships in the port. There were also many prostitutes.

I decided to travel through the Mersey Tunnel by bus, just because I had heard about it. It was just a brightly-lit tunnel under the river, but there was a lot of traffic. I had been told of a very good bed and breakfast place in Birkenhead, which catered for long-distance lorry drivers, so I went to Birkenhead next and stayed there. The place was neat and clean but in no way luxurious. The board was seven shillings and sixpence a day, which was very cheap. The breakfast was so good I have never forgotten it. Never again have I had such a good breakfast for so little cost. The other residents and I were given egg and bacon, but what a lot of bacon! Almost half a pound, I believe. We were also served chips and baked beans, then toast with butter, marmalade and tea. And all this so soon after a war!

I enjoyed my leave. Most of the time I just looked around different places, travelling by tram, bus and train. After the first holiday I visited these places from time to time. One day I was in Manchester when the weather became very drizzly, so I decided to see a movie. It was the sort that went on all day, the same pictures over and over again; they had a lot like that in those times. Once I was inside I found the place smelt vile and there was very poor ventilation; I could hardly see the screen for cigarette smoke. Many people were asleep and I concluded that homeless people came in when the weather was bad. It was two shillings to get in, and I enjoyed the film so I did stay, but I didn't like the smoke and smell and was sorry that picture houses were like that in England. I enjoyed going to films, even though I only knew a little English, but I still went to see films despite the smoke and the smelly theatre.

* * *

One Sunday I visited a church in Manchester. It belonged to the

Church of England, who rented it to the Ukrainian clergy and congregation for whatever days they needed it. I heard that they would rent it to any other Protestants, but not Catholics. The church was said to be over a thousand years old. It was cold, dark and dank and not a bit like the colourful Ukrainian churches I was used to. I heard that a very famous Archbishop was going to lead the service and I felt privileged to attend a service over which he would preside. His name was Archbishop Polikarp and he had been a priest for most of his life. He was over ninety years old and had been a prisoner of the Russians at one time. Some of his congregation had helped him escape to Poland and then to Western Germany. Much later he came to Britain. The church was very crowded so I only saw him from a distance. He was small in stature and dressed all in white. He had attendants to help him because of his advanced age.

A little later I decided to visit a different place and decided on the town of Chester. I bought a map and travel guide and managed to understand them enough so I could see around the place. The town had a thousand-year-old wall all the way around it, and this was the most interesting thing about Chester. The wall was very thick, like a road, and had protected the city in the very olden times. I walked all the way around the town on this wall. I found Chester a lot cleaner than Manchester but the streets were very narrow. It was obviously an old town and seemed to me as if it hadn't changed very much over the years.

* * *

In 1951, almost a year after I had been admitted to the hospital for the second time, I was discharged with a clean bill of health. I was also discharged from the Polish resettlement corps and was now a civilian. The PRC found me a job in an army camp at a place called

Nescliffe in Shropshire, which is midway between Shrewsbury and Oswestry. My new billet was a typical army Nissen hut with a rounded tin roof. The building was one very long room with a partition across the middle. I was billeted in one half with three men. Four other men lived on the other side. The four of us on my side were Ukrainians, but this seemed to have been a coincidence as they had come from different places and had not been in the PRC. Some were displaced persons from Germany. There was a coke stove for warmth and I had bought a frying pan to use on it. Although there was a canteen in the camp, I liked to cook for myself sometimes too, but we were not supposed to do so.

Although this was a British army camp where male and female soldiers were billeted, we civilians were allowed to live there in a separate area. The British called us EVWs — European Voluntary Workers. This seemed an incorrect name as we were paid a normal wage. I don't remember very much about two of the men in our section, but the other one I remember well as he was quite unusual. He was only nineteen, very tall and slim and would almost drown himself in expensive perfume. Most men didn't wear fragrances in those days. His name was Basil and the name seemed to suit him. He had an expensive-looking leather briefcase which he liked to show off and carry everywhere, however we would smile as we knew he only carried a toothbrush and paste in it and sometimes sandwiches. He imagined that people thought he carried important papers in it. He was not homosexual; he and his friend would go to Shrewsbury and stand on a certain street corner to watch girls go by.

My work at first was painting different areas of the camp when the weather was good. I also often worked in the ammunition depot. We didn't make ammunition, we inspected it, deciding if it was fit to be used again, sometimes dismantling it and cleaning it. It was very dangerous work because a lot of the ammunition was sent to us in very poor condition. In my spare time I would go alone to Shrewsbury or Oswestry to look around, window shop and go to the movies. I started going to wrestling bouts, but soon became disillusioned; I had hoped to see interesting scientific wrestling, but soon found out it was just a lot of show, noise and pretense so I stopped going. I decided it was time I bought another suit. I had saved enough money for one and by then didn't need coupons. I knew where there was a men's clothing shop in Shrewsbury where they made suits to measure, so I decided to have one made. I chose good medium brown material and went in a couple of times for fittings. It turned out to be a very smart suit, double breasted and fitting perfectly. It cost twelve pounds which wasn't cheap, but this suit was worth the price and I got years of wear out of it. I still have it today, although I don't wear suits now.

One day while I was shopping in Shrewsbury, I saw a very nice-looking camera in a shop window. I had always wanted to own a camera, so I went in and had a look at it. I really liked it and did have some extra money with me. It was an Italian camera called a Koroll and took 120mm films but had no flash so it was only for outdoor photos. It cost four pounds ten shillings, which was a whole week's wage for me, but it wasn't really expensive for a good modern camera. I decided to buy it and took it with me every time I went out. I liked to show my camera off. Much later I managed to buy a case for it.

* * *

There were a lot of female soldiers living on the camp. They were called WRACs, which stood for Women's Royal Army Corps. The other civilian men and I would try to pick these women up. We didn't have much success because their officers and the male officers warned them against us. I did manage to make a date

with a pretty, plump, smartly-dressed young WRAC girl called
Dorothy. Her nickname was Dot and as her surname was Tonks
so she was known as Dot Tonks which seemed a funny name
to me. On our first date we went to a movie in Shrewsbury. We
didn't even kiss. Our second date was in the evening. This time
we were not so formal and later we went to a cosy corner I knew
of behind a fence, where some Poles, including one crazy old man,
were billeted. Dot and I kissed and cuddled and after a while this
old man deliberately threw a bucket of cold water over the fence,
all over us. Although it may seem funny now, at the time I was
absolutely furious and Dot was very upset. I knew who had
done it and that it wasn't accidental. I didn't tackle him because
Dot didn't want any trouble. I apologised to her as I walked her
back to her billet and she said she had decided not to see me again
as a boyfriend, though I met her again later.

After Dot and I had parted, I heard that a new batch of women
soldiers had arrived at the camp. To get to their billets they had to
pass my door so I kept a look out for them. One day I was standing outside my door drinking milk when I saw a group of these
women on their way back from the canteen. I knew a few English
words by this time and said, 'Hello, would you like a drink of
milk?' Most of them ignored me but one very small woman, just
a girl really, stopped and said, 'No thank you, I don't like milk.'
She smiled and walked away.

The following Saturday I was in Shrewsbury looking around
the shops when I saw the same small young woman standing
alone in Woolworths drinking a soft drink. She looked very
young and small. She was also very blonde like my sister, Frossia.
I thought she looked like a baby bird that had just escaped from its
egg. I walked up to her and said, 'Hello, what's your name?' She
replied, 'Kathleen.' I told her that my mother's name was Katarina
and she said, 'My mother is Kathleen too.' I asked what she was

drinking and she replied, 'Ginger beer.' I asked her if she would like to go for a walk with me on the banks of the Severn River and she said she would. I was hoping for a permanent relationship with a nice girl. I thought, *I wonder if I have made a mistake. Maybe this isn't the woman for me.* Although she didn't know me and had only spoken to me once before, she hadn't hesitated in agreeing to go for a walk with me. Later I found out that she didn't like to say no in case I thought she didn't like foreigners.

As we walked along we came to a small fair. It had a round-about, a few rides and some sideshows and shooting galleries. I thought I would try my hand at shooting — I knew I was considered a good shot and wanted to show off in front of Kathleen. After I had paid, the man gave me a rifle and eight rounds of ammunition. I realised the rifle sights were incorrectly focused, but I compensated for this. When the man realised I was getting a good score he kept ducking under the rifle to put me off my aim. However, I did win a prize. I told Kathleen to choose something for herself to remember the day. She chose a medium-sized wall mirror with a green frame and seemed pleased with it. I agreed with her that it was the best prize there.

After that we walked along the banks of the Severn and came upon a man hiring out row-boats. I asked Kathleen if she would like to come out in a boat with me and she agreed but seemed very nervous. I asked whether she was afraid of water to which she replied, 'Who, me?' I found out later that she was very frightened of water. I had my camera with me and I asked the boat owner if he would take a couple of photos of us in the boat, then Kathleen and I took photos of each other. I rowed the boat out into the middle of the river. It was a small boat and very easy to handle. There was a great number of white swans on the river and we enjoyed looking at the scenery and talking. I understood a lot of what she said.

After a while I asked her if she would like to row, so she tried it for a while but had no idea how it should be done. I tried to show her, but she just rowed in circles. She also said more than once that she could not swim. So I took over the rowing again and rested the boat under the shade of some willow trees. We sat in the boat in the shade and talked for a while and then went back out into the middle of the river. We had been told not to go past a certain point so the man could call us in through a megaphone when our time was up. The time seemed to slip by very quickly and we were both sorry when we had to take the boat in. As neither of us had eaten, I would have liked to take her to a small, very nice Italian restaurant that I often went to called Sidoli's, but we didn't have time. She had to be back at the camp and we would have to catch the bus back. So I bought some bread, salami, gherkins and soft drinks and two small cakes. We enjoyed our meal sitting on the riverbank, then caught the bus back to camp. I asked her if she would like to come with me to Sidoli's the following Saturday. She said she would.

However, we didn't go to the Italian restaurant the following Saturday because the army had arranged a dance and expected all personnel to attend. The soldiers were allowed to bring whom they wished, although this wasn't always the case. We went to the dance and although I couldn't dance we had quite a good evening. Kathleen couldn't dance either, but she did go around the floor a couple of times with other men. We had some food and a cup of tea and talked together and with other people. Then we had a professional photo taken. Because we couldn't dance we left early and went for a long walk, then back to our billets. After this we started going out regularly. I often took her to Sidoli's, and she seemed surprised by how much I could eat. I really enjoyed their food and sometimes ordered both main dishes, as well as soup and dessert. She didn't eat very much but really enjoyed Sidoli's fish and chips. I preferred their real Italian dishes.

We often went window shopping in Oswestry or Shrewsbury and she liked going to the movies almost as much as I did. We would also go walking in the woods and I would bring an atlas of the world and show her different countries. Geography was something she knew very little about. I'd always been interested in it and would have liked to have been a cartographer if I had lived a normal life. I also taught her the Ukrainian alphabet from Ukrainian newspapers. She didn't talk very much to other people, but liked to talk to me and enjoyed teaching me English. I was eager to learn the English language and would bring an English/ Ukrainian dictionary with me when we met.

* * *

Kathleen had mentioned how poor the food in the army canteen was so I started to buy food for her. She liked garlic salami and pickled gherkins and pig trotters which I made myself. These were foods she had never even heard of before she met me. I was rather inclined to overdo things and often gave her too much food, especially pig's trotters in jelly in a dish or plate. She told me she couldn't eat it all and asked if I'd mind if she shared with the other girls in her billet. I didn't mind but nobody wanted this kind of food as it was not what they were used to, especially garlic. Kathleen had nowhere to put the food she couldn't eat, but as the weather was cool and most of the food was the sort that would keep fairly well, she made some space for it in one of her clothes drawers. One of the girls who was supposed to be a friend reported this to their sergeant, but couldn't resist telling Kathleen that she had done so. Kathleen ate what she could on the spot and threw the rest in the rubbish, including the plate. She hated wasting anything, especially food, so she was quite annoyed at having to throw good food away. She had intended to give it back to me the next day because she couldn't give it away.

When the sergeant came around to inspect the barracks she asked a few of the girls, including Kathleen, to open their chest of drawers and was surprised to find nothing but clothing in them. There was no rule against having food in the rooms but there would have been if she had found any. Kathleen asked the girl who had reported her if she had wanted her to get caught. The girl said yes, so Kathleen asked her why she had told her about it, giving her time to get rid of the food before the inspection. But it seemed the girl just wanted her to know she was the one who reported her and didn't seem to know why she hadn't waited until after the inspection to tell her, in which case Kathleen would have been in trouble. Kathleen decided to drop her as a friend and not only for this reason. She was becoming very odd, so I was told.

* * *

Kathleen and I really enjoyed each other's company and I thought it was about time we started having a love affair. But she was an innocent and wouldn't hear of it. I thought, she's very young, only eighteen, I'll wait, and after a few months I felt I was falling in love with her. One night I said, 'When are we going to get married?' She seemed surprised and said, 'Married?' as if she had never heard the word before. She didn't say yes or no but gave me the impression that the answer was yes. She said, 'I'm underage and I don't think my parents, especially my father, will agree.' I asked her if she would tell them when she wrote home. She did so.

Her father, who usually did the writing for the family, wrote back to say that they considered her to be too young to marry. They were also not happy that she wanted to marry a man they hadn't met and who was a lot older than her. I was twenty-nine years old and from a country they knew nothing about. Even though Kathleen had warned me that this was what they would say, I was disappointed. She was going home on leave at Christmas time and I asked her to try to speak to her parents. I told her that I didn't want any trouble with her parents, but as she was a very calm type of person I was sure she would not argue with them.

One evening I decided it would be fun to steal some pears from a tree that was very close to the road, but inside a farm property. Kathleen really hated this and was a very nervous, nagging, lookout. I stood on the fence and managed to pick about a dozen fruit. One other night we were sitting talking on the grass verge by the side of the road when a police car came along, shining a very strong light all around the area. We ducked behind a brick wall before they could see us. Kathleen was indignant and slightly annoyed that we were hiding when we had done no wrong, but at that time I was wary of police. Living so long under communism cannot be forgotten so quickly.

When the winter of 1952 arrived it was a very cold one. We had large black stoves in our billets for warmth and we had been provided with a quantity of coal. For some reason the women had not been issued with any and it seemed their frequent request for coal was ignored. They had started breaking up the small amount of furniture they had to use as fuel for the stoves. When they were not working or out, they would stay in bed with their clothes on and overcoats on top of the bed coverings to keep warm. After a while we found out that some of the women were dressing as men to enter our area, then climbing the fence where the coal was kept and stealing it. I spoke to Kathleen about it as I believed the culprits were from her billet, which had no coal at all. She didn't know they had been stealing and I asked her to tell the girls that we knew what they were doing and that some of the men were thinking of reporting them if they didn't stop. She thought they hadn't told her because they were stealing from the area where I lived, but when she spoke to them, it seemed that they hadn't considered her because she was too small to pass as a man and only the ones doing it knew about it.

When Christmas arrived and Kathleen prepared to go home on leave, I bought her some short black fur boots and a very nice scarf and a few other things for her birthday, which was two days after Christmas. I was pleased that she had bought me a present — a scarf and some gloves — because she had very little money and I really hadn't expected anything. I saw her off on the bus and reminded her to speak to her parents, wishing her and her family a Merry Christmas 1952 and Happy New Year 1953. When she arrived home she wrote me a short letter, knowing someone would read it to me. She didn't mention our wedding, but said she would talk to me when she got back. I decided to send her a birthday card and with help from one of the men, wrote her a short letter. I believe we still have this card and letter.

CHAPTER XVIII

Married life

IN early 1953 Kathleen arrived back in camp and told me her parents had not changed their minds. She suggested we wait, but I didn't want to wait and asked her to write again, enclosing a consent form I had picked up. One night as we were sitting in our clubroom, she said to me, 'I have a strong feeling there is something you haven't told me, but would like to.' I felt that this might be about my name change — it had been on my mind a lot — so I told her about it and why I had changed it. I said, 'If we get married, I would like to have my correct name and I would also like you and any children we have to be called Antonenko.' I also told her I had just recovered from TB.

Not long after this we were surprised to receive a letter from her father saying that her mother had persuaded him to consent to our marriage. They had also signed the consent form. Once we had the form we could plan the wedding. I asked Kathleen if she would mind being married in the Ukrainian Orthodox faith — she didn't, as she was also a Protestant. I travelled up to London to see Father Sergei Molchanivski, who was the Archbishop for all the Ukrainian Orthodox churches in Britain, to ask him about changing my name back again, getting a birth certificate because I couldn't be married without one, and arranging a date for our wedding.

For a small fee, the Father made a birth certificate for me and asked two men from the Ukrainian club to act as witnesses. He asked me a lot of questions and I had to admit I didn't know the day of my birth. He asked me if I had any idea of my birth date, and I said the beginning of September, as I remembered that it was often harvest time on my birthdays. He told me to choose a day and I decided on the fifth. I have never been sure why I picked five and since that time, I have always celebrated my birthday on the fifth of September. After he had made out my new birth certificate, the Archbishop told me to go to the CID at the police station in Oswestry to inform them of my real name and to get my name changed on my identity card. I had quite a lot of explaining to do as to why I changed my name in the first place, but eventually everything was settled and it cost nothing.

Once we had decided to be married I had asked Kathleen, whom I now called Katya, if she would mind being married in March, so I could get a good rebate from the taxation office, and she said, 'Why not?' But when I asked Father Molchanivski if we could be married in March he said he was very busy and all booked up and wouldn't be able to marry us until April 11th. When I returned from London, I discussed it with my fiancée and we decided we would be married on March 21st in the registry office in Oswestry, and then on April 11th by the Archbishop.

I wanted Katya to be married in white but it was very difficult to get the material, even though the war had been over for years. What little there was we couldn't possibly afford. It would have been so nice if I could have let my family know I was about to be married, but in those times it would have been very dangerous for them to receive a letter from the west, even if I had known where they lived and if a letter managed to get through. There was also a possibility that it could be dangerous for Katya and I and any family we might have. We would have liked Katya's family to come to our wedding but her mother wrote to say they could not afford the fare. We could only just manage to scrape up enough money for the first two weeks' rent for the rooms we would be moving into after our wedding, so we were sorry we couldn't help them with money either.

* * *

Katya had wanted to stay in the army but the authorities had suggested that it would be better to leave because she would have to sign on for another three years and wouldn't be released early unless she became pregnant. We thought about it and decided it was better not to be tied down by the army in case we wanted to move to places that didn't suit them, and we didn't know if we would be blessed with children. I had met a young Ukrainian man called Mike Turchin who lived in the barracks next to me with his father. We talked a lot and got on quite well. His English was very good and he would chat away to Katya when they met. His father spoke no English and was a very simple man of few words, even in Ukrainian. I thought at first that Mike was a very nice person, but there were times when he was very surly and I found that he was quite a heavy drinker. He worked in the ammunition depot too and after a while bought a motorbike. I considered him very careless with the bike and was quite worried when he gave Katya a lift after seeing her standing at the bus stop ready to return home. I told her how dangerous I thought he was when riding the bike. I thought she might not take notice of my advice but she did and never accepted another lift from him. She didn't tell me at the time but I guessed she must have already decided he was an unsafe rider.

I had a new medium-grey suit made for our wedding by the same tailors in Shrewsbury who made my brown one. It cost fourteen pounds but was worth it. The weather was cool and we couldn't get a wedding gown so we decided Katya should have a costume made. It was also grey and a shade lighter than mine. It was made by a private person, as the shop where my suits were made only catered for men. Her costume cost twelve pounds and seemed all right at the time of our first wedding, but later when we looked at the wedding photos we could see the skirt didn't sit right and was puckered on one side seam. Katya said the woman must have been trying to save material and had not cut it properly.

We had a choice of two types of flowers — orchids, which were expensive, or white or pink carnations. I wanted Katya to have the best flowers if she wanted them, but the orchids were brown with yellow spots and Katya said they would not suit our grey clothing. So we decided on pink carnations. The shopkeeper said he would make a spray of three with small fern leaves and silver foil for Katya and buttonhole flowers for everyone else. I asked Mike if he would be a witness at our registry office wedding and best man at the church wedding. I had also made friends with a shy, quiet, country boy called Nick whose other names I can't remember. I asked him if he would like to be a witness at the first ceremony and my groomsman at the second. He was very pleased to be asked. Katya asked Dot Tonks and another friend called Doreen Robinson to be witnesses and bridesmaids and another girl called Brenda to be a bridesmaid for the church wedding.

When the day of our registry office wedding came around, we all travelled to the office in Oswestry by taxi. It was very dull and uninteresting — not a bit the way I had always imagined my wedding would be and not like the weddings I remembered in Ukraine in the beautiful churches. We had a slight disagreement with one of the women clerks at the registry office, who kept on insisting that Katya was born in 1923 and not 1933, even though we showed her birth certificate and parent's permission paper. An official also asked me several times if I was sure I had not been married before. After the ceremony we went to the photographer's studio and even though we had an appointment and arrived on time, he was very nasty to us. I didn't know if this was because I was a foreigner or because we were married in a registry office and when Katya jokingly said to me in connection with one of the photos, 'You're too tall,' he very nastily said, 'You should have thought of that before.'

We took our witnesses for a meal to a cafe in Oswestry, then we took a taxi to the camp to take our guests home. These old type taxis had seats in the middle and back as well as in the driver's compartment. On the way back to camp I remember Katya sitting next to me in the middle looking very shy and putting her head down as we travelled through the camp with everyone looking at us. But in the back, with the other witnesses, Dot Tonks was leaning forward smiling and waving as if it were her wedding or she was royalty. After saying goodbye, we collected our few belongings and my bike to take to the rooms we had rented.

* * *

We had paid two weeks' rent for rooms in Oswestry with a young widow who told us to call her Eileen. I say rooms but it was really a bedroom; we shared the kitchen and I kept my bike in the corridor. We were quite happy there, although we couldn't afford to go away on a honeymoon. We had very little money. We both had two weeks' holiday so we enjoyed doing things like going to the movies, walking and also window shopping, as we had done before our wedding. We were both looking forward to our church wedding. We had hired the camp church for the ceremony and were going to wear the same clothes and have the same type of flowers made up for us.

I often showed Katya how to cook Ukrainian dishes and we got on very well. I thought that it was the start of a very normal, smooth way of life for me and my new wife. Then, to our surprise, after our rented time was up and we tried to pay the next week's rent, Eileen told us we must find somewhere else to live. We were shocked at having to move so soon and felt that we had done no wrong, so Katya asked her why she wanted us to go. She said, 'I'm fed up with the smell of onions, you do too much cooking with them.' We thought this was a poor reason, but didn't want to stay where we were not wanted. We said we would look for somewhere else to live. We looked around at several places, but had no luck.

* * *

One day we heard of a place not far away and because I considered my English not very good I suggested that Katya walk round to see the owners while I got the shopping in. When Katya told the woman of the house that I was Ukrainian, she said, 'Why did you marry one of those? Were you pregnant?' Katya said, 'No I was not, they are just the same as us only they speak a different language.' The woman then replied, 'You may think so, but I don't want any of them in my house.' We suspected other people we visited felt the same way, but she was the only one to insult us. We had to tell Eileen that though we wanted to leave, we couldn't find another place, but would keep trying. She then told us that there was an elderly unmarried woman living in the same street who sometimes let her top room. We would be able to share her kitchen and put my bike in the woman's small backyard if she agreed to have us. We went to see the old lady whose name was Nurse Jones. She agreed and told us we could move in anytime we liked. She said she was often away from home on private nursing jobs and sometimes stayed at an old friend's house. We could use her sitting room when she wasn't there.

* * *

The bedroom we were given was near the top of the house, up a lot of stairs, and the whole place except the kitchen, which was at the back of the house, was dark and gloomy. But she wasn't a bad sort of person and except for trying to get us to talk about our private life, she was okay. The first night we were there I wrote letters to thank my witnesses. Katya had already done her writing ages ago so she got into bed while I finished my letters. We were talking as I rested from writing, which is always a chore for me, when the bed suddenly collapsed. I thought, *the old woman can't look after the place properly.* I repaired the bed for her and us. The next day Katya told Nurse Jones the bed had collapsed and that I had repaired it. We were surprised to find that the old woman had fixed the bed to collapse as a honeymoon joke. We found her to be a bit odd and at times she would be very old-fashioned, telling Katya that as a married lady she shouldn't wear shorts, which she only wore around the house. At other times she would speak to us in a very bold cheeky way. But she was a lot nicer to us than Eileen had been.

Now that I was married and because most of the men were finding jobs outside the base, I looked around for a job and was surprised to find one in a plastic factory at Oswestry. I was lucky — there were very few jobs around for unskilled workers, especially foreigners. The pay wasn't very good, but I sometimes managed to work overtime.

When our church wedding day arrived we walked from our lodgings to the flower shop and after picking up all the flowers, we took a taxi to the army base. When we arrived, Katya visited her bridesmaids to give them their flowers. I went around to see if Mike and Nick were ready and to give them their buttonholes. It occurred to me that they had the same names as my two friends in my home village in Ukraine. The Archbishop and his assistants were already at the church which was a round army Nissen hut.

They were preparing for the ceremony as best they could. Katya had been discharged from the army but they didn't mind us hiring the church. We all assembled outside Katya's friends' billets and when we were all ready we walked the short distance to the church. Someone said to me, 'You shouldn't see the bride on your wedding day until you get to the church.' I smiled; this would have been very difficult to achieve, having travelled to the base together, and of course we were already married. I had kept in touch with Inas Omilianenko, who I had met in hospital, and had written and asked him if he would be my best man, before I asked Mike. I can't remember why he couldn't come, but I remember he would have liked to. I know he had a very good reason for not coming. I just can't remember what it was.

When we arrived at the open church door our attendants walked to the front of the church and sat down while we waited in the doorway. Usually in Ukrainian churches there are no pews, only a few benches around the walls for the elderly. However, this Nissen hut had been converted into an English church and had seating. In a few minutes Father Mochanivski greeted us and turning, led us to the altar. I had already bought white candles, white material and a white towel for the ceremony and left them with the Father. We stood upon the towels and were given a candle each to hold. The priest's attendants gave Mike and Doreen, who was Katya's chief bridesmaid, a crown each to hold over our heads for the length of the very long service. It must have been difficult for Mike as he was shorter than me, but he didn't say anything. For certain parts of the service our candles were lit and when we walked around the altar with the white cloth tied around our hands our attendants held those candles. The priest tells and asks the bride and groom the same things as in the English service, such as be faithful, promise to be together for life and to look after each other in sickness and health. Because Katya couldn't speak Ukrainian the Father put her answers in for her. It meant a lot to me that she was very willing to be married in the Ukrainian church. Some of my friends took photos of the service, which turned out very well. We didn't bother to have professional photos taken, as we had the ones from our registry office wedding and we couldn't really afford any more.

After the ceremony and congratulations, the three girls threw confetti over us and took more photos outside the church. Then all our guests made excuses, saying they had to go for various reasons. I knew they were going over to a large hall that they had hired from the army to prepare a reception for us. My friends had spoken to Katya's friends and they had agreed that a reception party would be a good wedding present for us. They had put their money together and when they told me their plans I had added some money too. Katya knew nothing of this and was preparing to go home, so I told her I wanted to visit some other friends first. As we walked over to the hall, she said suspiciously, 'Who do you know living over here?' Before I needed to answer, two of my friends came from around the hall and opened the two large doors, revealing long tables laden with food and drink. All our friends were standing with their glasses raised to us. Katya looked absolutely stunned — she really hadn't expected anything — and we had a wonderful reception party. I translated good wishes to Katya from the Bishop and the Ukrainians whose English was poor. Everyone laughed when Dot Tonks wanted a cup of tea, the only beverage not included in the party, so someone went over to the army kitchen to bring some.

When we finally arrived home at our rooms, Nurse Jones (we never knew her first name) gave us a very fine tablecloth. We were very pleased as we had not expected the old lady to give us anything. A few days later a very nice dinner and tea set arrived from Katya's family. Her father wrote a letter congratulating us on behalf of the family, saying her mother had picked the present and he had carefully packed it. I was happy that they had accepted me.

* * *

After a while Katya decided to try to get a job, hoping that we might be able to save a little money from two wages. She went to the Labour Exchange and was told she would never get a job with "a surname like that". However, they did send her around to a few places. Eventually she was offered a job at a small cafe called the Coach and Dogs. She told me it was a very old and historic place and quite pleasant. She liked the look and feel of it. One of the elderly women owners, whose name was Miss Bull, said to Katya, 'I like you and will give you the job because your maiden name was Bull.' Katya thought it was disgraceful that people liked or disliked you, or decided if you could have a job, because of your name. However, she took the job because there was nothing else. She didn't mind the work. Sometimes she was a waitress and at other times she did odd jobs, depending on how busy they were.

* * *

We were still living at Nurse Jones' place when we received a letter from one of Katya's sisters, the youngest of the twins named Jean. She asked if she could stay with us for a few days — she had managed to save a small amount of money for the train fare. We asked Nurse Jones and she said she would be pleased to allow Jean to visit and could find her a bed for a couple of days at no charge. We were happy about Jean visiting us — I hadn't met any of Katya's family. When she arrived we enjoyed taking her out shopping in Oswestry and Shrewsbury. We treated her to the pictures and also took her out in a rowboat on the River Severn. I'm not sure now, but I believe it was the weekend. I, of course, took my camera along and took a lot of photos. We also took a lot of photos in Nurse Jones' backyard.

Katya wanted children as soon as possible. Although I had always wanted children, especially sons, I did not think that this was a good time — it was much too soon. We didn't have our own place or much of anything and there was very little room where we lived. I felt that we couldn't afford a child yet. But Katya believed she was an unlucky person and thought that perhaps she wouldn't be able to have children. She wanted to find out as soon as possible. 'Everything will be all right, we will manage, we won't die,' she said. So we decided to see if God would send us any children and did not try to prevent pregnancy.

* * *

We had been married about four months when Katya told me she was absolutely sure she was pregnant. She had visited a doctor and although in those days the doctors could not tell until three months had gone by, she was certain she was right. I started to worry, thinking what a big step having a child was when we were not prepared. I thought Katya was too young to have thought this through and that I should have been more responsible.

But I really wanted a child. How nice it would be to have a family of our own. Katya's parents were delighted at the thought of becoming grandparents for the first time and when we told Nurse Jones she was pleased too. We told her we thought we would have to look for another place as there was very little room at her place, especially for a pram. She seemed genuinely sorry to hear that we would be leaving and told us we could have her attic at no extra charge if we couldn't find somewhere else. We were pleased that she liked having us there. We didn't tell her we considered the place too dark and damp for a new baby. We looked around but had no luck finding a place to live.

When Katya was two and a half month's pregnant we heard there was going to be a big song and dance festival, called an Eisteddfod, in Llangollen, over the border in North Wales. There would be groups of dancers and singers from many countries of the world, including Ukraine, who were now living in Britain. As it was to be held on a Saturday, we decided to go. It meant we would have to be up very early to travel by public transport and we would be out all day, but Katya had been keeping very well and wanted to go. We took some sandwiches and drinks and started out. The event was held on a very large piece of land and a huge tent was used as the concert hall. We were very disappointed at first as there were so many people we could not see a thing. Katya got quite irritated saying, 'We have come all this way for nothing.' She started to feel unwell and I thought we might be having a problem with the baby, but after sitting on the grass for a while and having a drink and some food, she seemed to be as well as ever. Some of the groups, realising that many people had missed out, sang and danced for the people outside which was very good of them; it wasn't part of their scheduled routine. We had a very good day after all and Katya seemed her own self again. We both took lots of photos of the performers.

CHAPTER XIX

Family man

F ROM the time she realised she was pregnant until a short time before the baby was born, Katya suffered from morning sickness every day, and not only in the mornings. But apart from this she kept quite well and wanted to keep working at the Coach and Dogs. Nurse Jones gave us advice on pregnancy; she was happy at the thought of a baby and sorry that we wanted to move, but we felt that we needed a larger, lighter more modern place to live before the baby arrived. When Katya was about four months pregnant, an Irish friend, Kevin Munster, who worked at the same place as me, and who had tried to help us before, told me that a family living on the other side of Oswestry were prepared to let two rooms in their home. He had spoken to them about us and they didn't mind that we were expecting a child as they had two children of their own.

We went over to look at the place. The rooms looked all right and the woman who showed us around seemed pleasant. One of the rooms was downstairs next to the kitchen and the other upstairs room was quite large and would be our bedroom if we decided to rent the rooms. We felt that it wasn't a bad place and the rent was reasonable so we paid a deposit. After telling Nurse Jones, we started moving our few belongings to our new rooms. One problem was that our old rooms had been furnished, but the new rooms were not. We didn't want to spend money on furniture, because we wanted to save as much money as possible for a pram, cot and other things that the baby would need, so the woman and her husband said they could let us have a small table and two chairs for the downstairs room and a double bed and wardrobe with drawers for the upstairs room. I would carry one or both chairs up or down stairs as needed. We bought a few orange boxes to use as seats and cupboards. I also made bookshelves from boxes and we draped materials around some of our special furniture.

Katya had booked into the hospital months ahead; we had to do this because we were on the National Health Scheme. Her bosses at the cafe said they couldn't allow customers to see a pregnant woman so she was given jobs, such as clearing the back stairs and other out of the way areas. Then a long time before it was really necessary they sacked her, saying they couldn't have a pregnant woman around the place. Katya was extremely happy about being pregnant, so this didn't please her. She wasn't very big at that time, not until about seven and a half months, when she seemed to become as round as she was tall.

When Katya was forced to leave the cafe she joined pre-natal classes. I thought I should go too but the times were difficult because I was working, then I found out that they didn't allow husbands to attend. Throughout the pregnancy Katya developed a craving for fresh peaches, a fruit she didn't normally like. They were extremely expensive at half a crown (which was two shillings and sixpence) for one fruit. She said that was what the baby wanted and was going to have. We would laugh saying, 'What expensive tastes this child has.' Katya took extremely good care of herself for this baby and she would be teased by friends about this being the next heir or heiress to the throne. We both wanted a boy, but didn't really mind a girl as long as the child had nothing wrong with it.

We started thinking of names and as we would have the baby christened in my church and faith, I wanted the name of one of our saints, which is an Ukranian custom. I read out the possible names to my wife but we just couldn't agree. She said that to have a child called some of the names I liked would be a fate worse than death for the child. In the end I said, 'If I can name this child, you can name the next one.' I decided on the name Petro, which translates to Peter in English, for a boy and Katerina for a girl. Katya said, 'I really like the name Katerina, both our mothers have similar names and if the baby is a boy we can christen him Petro, but I will always call him Peter.'

* * *

Once we had settled in to our new rooms, Katya said she found our landlord's wife very difficult to live with. I thought Katya might just be going through a trying time being pregnant; I knew by now that she was rather a recluse, who liked to be alone or only with her family when at home. However, after a while I realised Katya was right and the woman was deliberately being difficult in subtle ways. We gave her the nickname Vidma, which means "witch" in Ukranian. She would use all the gas rings just when it was time for Katya to make or warm up my meals. Although we had our own clothes line, she would take our clothes down while they were still wet and sometimes turn the gas or electricity off, which could be done with the old type meters. I don't know why she did these things but there were so many instances that we couldn't be mistaken. We can't remember now all the things she did but it was very irritating and must have been more difficult for Katya, who had to spend more time around the house than I did. If we mentioned any of these incidents she would always have an innocent explanation. She would also try to listen to our conversations. Then she started trying to frighten my wife by telling her that if either of us had any illnesses in the past the baby would be born dead or blind. I thought if she knew I'd had TB she might throw us out.

When Katya got a very light electric shock, Vidma said the baby would only have one arm. So when Katya slipped and fell in the snow, we made sure that Vidma didn't know about it! I wanted to tell the woman off about these things, but Katya didn't want any trouble; tenants had no rights at all in those days. Katya said she didn't believe what Vidma was saying and was absolutely convinced that our baby would be perfect. However, I asked her to speak to her doctor next time she went for a check-up, and he said, 'Don't listen to these foolish old wives' tales.'

* * *

We had both been working for a while and had saved money for the baby's needs and as Christmas 1953 was drawing closer, we decided to visit Katya's family after they wrote to invite us. Because her father was in the army and the family moved quite often, they were now living closer to us. I was quite excited and wondered how an English family lived. It was a long time since I'd been with a whole family of people. The only way we could travel was by train. Katya wasn't having much trouble with her pregnancy and although we had to change trains, we experienced a normal uneventful journey.

We arrived on Christmas Eve day and left on December 30th, so Katya also spent her 20th birthday with her family. When we arrived we found all the family had also come for Christmas. Katya's family had a fairly large home, but her mother and father gave us their bed and slept in the sitting room on the floor. We said we would sleep on the floor, but they insisted that it was no hardship and that as Katya was pregnant we should have the bed. On Christmas Day they had all the usual Christmas festivities.

Although they had a roast and all the trimmings for the midday Christmas meal, I found that everything else was sweet food. There was so much sweet stuff that I was glad we had brought some salami and gherkins with us. Her family loved these foods, which were new to them, and wanted more. We couldn't get any salami where they lived, so we sent them some through the post when we returned home. As it wasn't far and salami keeps well, it travelled all right.

I got on very well with her family and found her mother an especially nice person. I enjoyed being there but remember being embarrassed when I tried to eat the decoration on top of the cake and found it was inedible, but nobody seemed to care. The young girls of the family were thrilled that we were expecting a baby and one of the Christmas presents was a very nice baby's photo album. Katya's youngest sister, Joan, was only about seven or eight years old and a charming, friendly little girl who was full of energy. She would ask me to play and tell me stories and sit on my knee. I thought her a very nice child and looked forward to my own child's birth time.

When we returned to Vidma's place it was quite an anti-climax, because she hadn't changed and was still making life difficult for us. She was a strange person; from time to time she would be kind to us, then go back to being difficult. We had our names down for a council house but didn't expect to get a place for years. We had tried to find somewhere else to live but it was obvious that Katya was pregnant and that I was a foreigner, so no one wanted us. I must have ridden my bike hundreds of miles, looking for a place to rent, so there was nothing to do but put up with it. We couldn't go back to Nurse Jones' place — she had let her rooms to someone else, but she was sorry we were having problems.

Doctor Green told us the baby was due to arrive on April 27th. We both hoped it would be a boy and I was absolutely sure of it so we bought mostly blue clothing, covers and toys. We also had a blue baby bath and a cot with blue pictures on it. Katya wanted a small pram, but I insisted that our child must have the very best pram and one big enough for me to push easily. I said we could also use it for any other children we might have. So we bought a "pedigree pram" which was a famous brand at that time. Katya was not sure about this — she didn't want to be seen to be showing off — and said, 'It looks like a boat,' but it was a beautiful pram, really. It cost about twenty-four pounds, quite expensive.

On April 19th she went into labour. Not knowing very much about babies, I was afraid that the child might fall on the floor and hurt itself, but both Katya and Vidma told me that this wouldn't happen. Vidma even phoned for a taxi and let the hospital know Katya was on her way. She even allowed Katya to take her phone number to give to the people at the hospital so they could call to let me know when the baby arrived and if everything was okay.

For the three days I waited for the baby's arrival, I continued to go to work at the plastic factory. Everyone knew we were about to have a baby and one of my bosses called me in to his office and said, 'When your wife and baby come home you can have a week off with pay.' He also said that as soon as the baby arrived, I could leave work to visit the hospital. I was very grateful as I hadn't asked for time off. While Katya was in hospital I went to the English Church to pray to God for the safety of my wife and child. I don't think much of the English churches; most of them, including this one, were dark, damp and musty, but I had an overwhelming feeling that everything would be all right, even though, because of the sort of life I've been forced to lead, I usually didn't expect the best. (I learnt later that they thought the baby was dead because it didn't cry.) While I waited, I was calm and believed all would be well. For me having a child was very important — it would be a whole new life; the sort of life a man should live.

On the morning of April 21st, Vidma telephoned me at work to say that the hospital had called. Katya and I had a healthy 7lb 3oz baby boy and his mother was also doing well. My bosses allowed me to leave straight away and as visiting hours were not until later, I shopped around for some gifts to take to the hospital for Katya. I bought chocolates and grapes and a pineapple — the latter two being expensive luxuries in Britain at that time. I could hardly wait to see them and see what my new son looked like. I was so happy I wept.

The hospital was a maternity hospital only and quite small. When I arrived at the hospital, after I had given my name, one of the nurses said, 'Your baby looks just like you.' When I was shown to the ward I noticed that all the babies were with their mothers and that there were eight beds in all. I was a bit shy and went over to give Katya her gifts. When I gave her a kiss she said, 'The baby looks just like you.' I thought the nurse said that too, but people always say something like that — I guessed that such young babies didn't really look like anyone — so I was very surprised when I saw him for the first time. He had dark brown hair and his dark blue eyes were open and although I thought how small he was, he really did look like my father's side of the family. I was so happy I could feel tears flowing down my face. *A perfect child*, I thought.

When I arrived home I thanked God that my wife and child were safe and well. The hospital staff kept them there a few days and in the meantime Katya wrote me a letter saying the baby was okay and that they had been moved to a different ward. By this time we had definitely decided to call our new son Petro. The second time I visited them the nurse said, 'Your baby screamed all last night and kept all the other babies awake.' Katya told me that one of the nurses had carried him all around the wards to show everyone because he was the only one with dark hair and the only boy.

She said this was very strange, as her mother had told her years ago that Katya had been carried around to be shown to all the ladies because she was the only fair-haired one and the only girl.

Katya and Petro would be coming home in a few days and we talked about this. She said, 'I don't want to bring him home to that place'. I was sad to hear this as I felt the same way. It wasn't the way I'd imagined it would be for my children. She saw I was sad and said, 'I'm sorry I said that — maybe things will be better now we have a child.' Vidma had been quite helpful just before Katya went into hospital and we both thought that if she liked children we might all be treated better. Just before leaving hospital the baby developed what everyone thought was a cold in the eyes. However, they allowed them to come home, saying it had almost cleared up.

Before they came home I went out and bought a new brightly coloured bed cover. Katya noticed this; she liked it and realised it was my small token to make arriving back a bit better. Unfortunately, as soon as Vidma saw Petro (whom we now called Peter), she didn't like him — he was a handsome boy, and as her children were not, especially the little boy, we guessed that she was jealous. She didn't say any of the nice things people say about babies, so Katya asked her, 'What do you think about the baby?' Vidma replied, 'He's very ugly, he's got his father's big nose and he can't open his eyes properly.' Things got worse and she gave us a very hard time. One of the worse things she did was try to stop us from having any warmth for Peter when he had his baths, even though she thought — as we did — that he had a cold in his eyes. In those days babies were bathed every day and there was no way of heating the downstairs room. But she insisted that we couldn't have water upstairs. Katya would wait until I came home and we would sneak the water upstairs every day. She never caught us. Often she would be next door at her friend's place, and this gave us our chance.

The woman who lived next door was very common, or "ocker" as Australians say. But she didn't take any notice of us. Vidma's husband was a very nice man, but totally under her control, and spoke very little. Vidma would give her little boy beer and wine and laugh when he staggered — he was only about four years old. We were getting desperate when I heard about a cottage for sale. It was fifteen miles away, out in the country, and miles from anywhere. We thought that this would be very inconvenient, but anything would be better than what we were putting up with. I could see Katya going from a calm person into a nervous wreck. When she came home from hospital she couldn't feed Peter breast milk, which we both would have liked for him, so we had to get up in the middle of the night to make his formula. He cried and screamed a lot and had more trouble with his eyes. Although the nurse came to see him, and we took him to doctors they were unable to help or tell us what was wrong. We could only bathe his eyes and try to comfort him by cuddling him. It was also very difficult to get nappies dry, but we worked hard trying to do our very best for our little boy.

We talked about the cottage and decided to go and look at it, even though we had very little money. The owner took us to see it in his car. We took Peter with us — Vidma offered to look after him but this was the very last thing we would have thought of doing. We didn't know if she was that bad but we didn't want Peter to have an "accident". We got a shock when we saw the cottage. It was terrible — not the way anyone would imagine a cottage to be. It was made of very large stones and looked like a very long stable. It had a lot of separate rooms and it was one of these rooms the man was trying to sell us. We noticed that some of the other rooms were taken, each family having only one room each. We couldn't believe that anyone would buy them, as the one we saw was very poor. The situation was ridiculous, because he wanted 700 pounds — a fortune in those days when most working men, including myself, earned six to eight pounds a week. We didn't say "no" in case he wouldn't give us a lift back home — we just said we would have to think more about it. Vidma or not, we couldn't take that cottage.

* * *

Just after this Katya thought she was pregnant again. We were devastated — we wanted more children, but at this time it would have been a disaster. Our doctor told her he believed that she was not expecting and that the problem could be stress. It was a terrible time for us, until it turned out the doctor was right. Katya's sister, Jean, was on her way to America to be a children's nanny and dropped in unexpectedly to say goodbye. She was shocked to see the way we had to live and was upset by the things we told her. Vidma was quite dirty and Katya had become fed up of cleaning up after her, so we were embarrassed that Jean saw the place in such a mess, but she could see our area and the baby were well kept. We had hoped to keep our situation from Katya's family so we asked Jean not to mention our circumstances. She said she hoped things would get better for us and our new son.

When Peter was six months old we decided it was time to have him christened. Father Molchanivski, who had married us, said he would visit us to conduct the ceremony if our landlady would allow it. To our surprise Vidma agreed. Later she told us she was very curious about what would happen. I had kept in touch with Inas, who was now married, so I asked if he and his wife would like to be Peter's godparents. He agreed and so it was arranged. Vidma had allowed us to use the upstairs room. Father did not bring any assistants and travelled by train. Inas and Cecilia, his wife, also travelled by train. Inas brought his modern cameras to take photos of the service, of Peter and of us. Cecilia handmade and embroidered a long white silk gown for Peter as a christening present from them both. Everything went well, but we could hear Vidma and her friend from next door laughing very loudly downstairs, but everyone ignored that. We found out later that they were laughing at the christening service, which had a certain amount of religious singing in it.

* * *

Sometimes Katya would put Peter outside the front door in his pram because the backyard was too cluttered to have room for a pram. One day she was on her way to see if Peter was all right, when she noticed that Vidma and her friend had taken his nappy off and were looking at and talking about his private parts. Katya told them she wasn't very pleased about this. They laughed at her saying, 'We were only saying good things about him.' When I came home from work Katya told me she was upset about this. I asked her if they had touched him and she said, 'I'm sure they didn't — I could see them as I was walking towards them.' She went on to say she didn't like them doing something that the child would object to if he could. I asked her if I should speak to them about it and she said, 'Yes.' I thought I would quietly ask them not to do it again because we didn't like it. So when the other woman came over to see Vidma, I asked if I could come into Vidma's sitting room and started to explain. I thought they might say sorry and that they wouldn't do it again but the other woman started screaming and making a big fuss and before I realised it we were having a tremendous row. I was so angry I threatened to call the police. This frightened everyone except Katya, who knew I wouldn't. In those days, the thought of anyone knowing that the police had been called to their house was embarrassing — even for people such as these.

The next day I wanted to apologise to Vidma's husband because the disturbance had occurred in his house. Although she was very shy, Katya said she would tell him and Vidma that we were both sorry. Katya and Vidma's husband had looked appalled at the time it happened and even Vidma was shocked. Later Katya told me that Vidma and her husband were surprised that we bothered to apologise, even agreeing it was the other person's fault. But the next day Vidma told us we would have to find another place to live. Katya said, 'Didn't you agree that it was really your neighbour's fault?' Vidma answered, 'Yes but I've got to live next door to her.' I started frantically looking for another place to live. I went everywhere on my pushbike. I worked at a very good place and many people there tried to help me. But when I enquired at the places they had suggested, other people insulted me, often saying, 'Go home to your own country.'

At this time Katya heard of a Swedish woman who had threatened to go back to Sweden, leaving her English husband and children, because they were having problems similar to ours and could find nowhere to live. The authorities in those days believed in keeping families together, so gave them a council house. Katya said to me, 'I don't like to do this but I'm going to try something. I'm going to see the council's health inspector nurse. I'll take Peter with me and I will tell her everything. Of course I can't say I'm going to another country as the Swedish woman did, but I'll say that I'm at the end of my tether and am going to leave you, taking the baby and going home to my parents. I'll try to bluff them into thinking that because my parents live in a force house, the army wouldn't allow you to live there.'

In reality, Katya's parents wouldn't have been able to manage Katya and the baby full-time but I agreed it was worth a try. On the day she decided to go, Vidma had upset her in some way, so when she talked to the nurse she was genuinely upset; as she told all our troubles she really cried. The nurse said that the council's members would discuss our case and be in touch with us. When Katya told me what happened I decided to do my bit. I went in and told someone on the council that I was going to kill myself. Little did they know that I would never kill myself. I had struggled to stay alive my whole life. I also knew Katya had no intention of leaving me, so these tactics may seem underhanded, but we were desperate. We didn't know if all this would result in them finding us a place to live, so I continued to look around.

* * *

One day I had ridden about four miles and came to a small village called Whittington. I asked at a few houses if they knew of a place that my family could rent. I had no luck for a while, then a man came up to me as I got off my bike and asked if I was the one looking for rooms. When I said I was, he said, 'See that long place like a mansion? That is called a Rectory and the religious leader who lives there sometimes lets some of the rooms.' I knocked on the huge front door which was opened by a middle-aged woman. I asked if they were letting rooms. She said, 'Yes, we do have two empty rooms which we are willing to let.' She showed me the rooms; they looked okay, but I would have taken anything at that time. When I got back and told Katya I had found somewhere for us, but that it was a little way out from town, she was very relieved to be leaving Vidma's place. She said she thought we would never get away, even though Vidma had asked us to go. We were so happy to be going. We really lived too close to Vidma and her family, a thing neither of us liked, even with good people. Her children would also sometimes get into our things as there were no keys to our area. Once the little girl squeezed toothpaste all over some oddments we had on a small table. They were only kids, but she never tried to stop them.

* * *

We moved into the Rectory as soon as we could. The rooms were
unfurnished but we had a small amount of furniture — some
I had made myself. We were given two rooms; a large passage
and a bathroom with a toilet. (We had to share these facilities
at Vidma's. She complained once about Katya having to go to
the toilet at night when she was expecting Peter, even though
she had children of her own. We hadn't been able to bathe Peter
in the bath with us and there was no way of heating that room.)
After a few days we found that the Rectory rooms were large,
high, old and very damp. We also found that the Rector was a
very nastily-spoken man who insulted me every time we met. He
was nicer to Katya but he didn't do anything spiteful like Vidma
had. Our quarters were quite separate so we didn't see him very
often. His wife was quite different — a real lady. We were able
to have warmth for Peter's bath time much more easily and I put
blankets around the outside of his cot to keep the draught out.

Besides the Rector, his wife and us, there was another young
couple living in a different part of the Rectory. We hardly ever
saw them; only occasionally did we exchange greetings such as
'Good morning'. The Rector told Katya that the couple argued
quite a lot but we only heard them once, when all the windows
were open on a fine day. Peter's eyes cleared up so well it was as
if he had never had any trouble with them, but he wasn't a good
baby and cried a lot, although we did our best to keep him happy
and comfortable. The other occupants of the Rectory were not
disturbed by his crying as the old walls were so thick. We still had
to make his formula in the middle of the night. I can't remember
if there were any fridges at that time but if there were, only very
rich people would have had them, so we couldn't make his milk
ahead of time. We had difficulty getting clothing dry, especially

nappies, and drying indoors made the place even damper. However, things were a lot easier for us than they had been at Vidma's and Katya seemed to be recovering from the experience.

CHAPTER XX

The country life

WE had only been in the Rectory a few weeks when a doctor from the health centre visited us. 'This place is much too damp for a young baby,' she said. She also asked us what complaints we had. We explained that our problems had happened at the other place and that we hadn't been at the Rectory very long. Almost one month later, the Rector told us he had taken a phone call from a member of the council to say we had been allotted a council house. About a week later we received a letter confirming this, telling us the address and asking us to drop in to the council offices to pick up the keys for the house. The letter explained that we were allotted the house because the Rectory was so damp. We went to see the house which was on very high ground, which we later christened "The Hill". It was in Whittington and was newly-built. It was very large and much too big for us but we definitely were not complaining about this; we were very happy to have a place by ourselves. When we were at the Rectory, I had to ride my bike to work a lot further than from Vidma's and now I would have to ride even further; four miles each way. But we did consider ourselves to be very lucky to be in this house.

Because I was working I didn't meet any of the village people but Katya, despite being very shy, did chat to the shopkeepers and would often hear gossip and happenings of the village. One day she told me about a family who had been living in the back of an old castle (which was a landmark in Whittington, but not open to the public). They were very upset that we had been given a house when they believed it to be their turn. We were sorry to hear this, but couldn't do anything about it. It wasn't very long before they also received a house, but later they took their revenge on us. We didn't have very much furniture, but what we did have was neat second-hand furniture, not orange boxes. We put some carpet down and curtained windows of some of the rooms. We lived in the parts of the house we could more easily keep warm and began to settle in. It was a bit difficult living on The Hill, especially in winter when it was hard to get in to the village and also very slippery for the delivery people. But being high up, the clothing dried more quickly than in other areas. In bad weather we dried nappies in front of the fire in the kitchen, with a fireguard as protection.

We were really happy to have a house to ourselves but it was very difficult for me to travel to the factory on my pushbike. There was no other transport for me to that area. In the winter it would be very cold, with snow and rain and the cold wind always seemed to be against me when I rode to work in the morning. By the afternoon the wind had usually changed direction and I would be heading into it coming home. I wore the fisherman's type oilskins of leggings, cape and sou'wester hat, rubber boots and also gloves. By the time I arrived at work and later home, I would be covered in sweat. To make things worse, Peter cried a lot at night. I would often sleep downstairs on the floor on a mattress so I could get some rest and be fit to go to work the next day. I liked working at the plastic factory and there was no chance of me getting another job in that area, so I had to put up with the difficult travelling.

When Peter started on semi-solid food, he really thrived and we thought he was a lovely boy. He was quite heavy and looked very healthy. He didn't walk until he was nearly two, which caused a few difficulties; he was a well-built heavy boy for Katya to carry. We would put him in his pram outside the back door to get fresh air when the weather was good. He was clever and would open the straps holding him in the pram even if we fastened them behind his back. He also shook his pram so hard it would move — even with the brake on — so we tied it to a water pipe. Even so, he still shook it loose. One day I heard one of our neighbours shouting and I ran out to find Peter's pram running across our garden to the garden at the back — there were no fences. I managed to catch the pram before any worse mishap occurred. After that I bought some planks from my factory and brought them home on my bike. I built a fence and with the spare pieces built a swing for my son.

Peter didn't bother to speak, either, until he was nearly two. He and Katya had a type of rapport; they understood each other without him having to speak. The lady doctor who visited us from time to time asked Katya if she thought he was normal. Katya had no doubts that not only was he normal but also very bright. Once he started speaking, he spoke perfect English, no baby talk. Katya thought he was so wonderful she wanted another baby, especially as we had a house to ourselves. I wasn't sure — I really wanted more children but we had gone through a lot.

Peter still had trouble with his eyes every April, near the time of his birthday. The doctors had at last told us it was a rare type of allergy called spring catarrh. It caused lumps to form on the inside of his eyelids, which irritated the eyeballs. We took Peter to a large clinic where the doctor we saw called other doctors in to examine Peter's eyes, saying, 'I bet you've never seen the likes of this before!' But they couldn't ease his suffering and it was very irritating and painful for him. It was awful not being able to do very much for him. We were given drops to put in his eyes and we would bathe them, but it only helped a little. Sometimes the allergy would cause him to try to bang his head on the wall in pain, but we always stopped this. Often pus would run from his eyes. We could only wait for the season to pass; it usually didn't last long. We thought it might be caused by grass or flower pollen, but the doctors were unable to confirm this. So we tried to keep him indoors at that time of the year — especially if it was windy.

I wasn't sure if we could afford another baby, but Katya really wanted one. We had no washing machine and we knew Katya wouldn't be able to breastfeed the child, so there would be some problems. I also wanted another child — I wasn't getting any younger and Katya said because she had a difficult time when Peter was born, she thought if we didn't decide soon she might lose her nerve and never want to go through another pregnancy. She wrote and told her family and her mother wrote back, asking if we were sure that we wanted another child so soon. We decided that we did and that it might as well be then — it was possible that we would never be able to really afford another child. Once we decided that was what we wanted, we were disappointed that Katya didn't become pregnant. She decided to speak to our doctor, who told us the best time of the month to try for a baby. We wanted a child in the springtime, as Peter had been, because there was a better chance of good weather to come as the child grew up.

* * *

After a while we were happy to find that we were going to have another child. Although I really liked working at the plastic factory, I was earning only about eight pounds a week. Sometimes I worked an extra four hours on Saturdays when they needed me, making it nine pounds. Considering that we were expecting another child, I wished I could get another higher-paying job, but there were no jobs around that area. With this pregnancy, Katya became very heavy very quickly, making everything difficult for her, especially pushing a big pram, looking after Peter and living on high ground. As Katya became even plumper she couldn't sit properly and I had to roll her out of bed in the morning, which made us laugh most of the time.

One day we walked in to Oswestry, which was four miles away, and on the way back Katya said, 'I can't walk another step.' She rested on the grass, then couldn't get up and had great difficulty walking. I was very worried — we had Peter in the pram and there was no way I could carry her, she was so heavy. I just had to keep encouraging her and stopping to rest. It took ages to get home and I was very anxious, saying, 'Come on, a few more steps then you can rest for a while. Soon we'll be home and you can go to bed.' To try to cheer her up I said, 'Come on, get up or I will have to roll you along.' There were very few houses around and hardly any traffic and they couldn't have helped because we had the pram. We just had to get home.

A short time after this Katya's father and her brother, John, travelled for almost a whole day on their bikes to see us and stay for a couple of days. It really was a big effort on their part; it took them another whole day to travel back. Katya was so large by then that her father thought she might be expecting more than one child as there are twins in their family. When they had returned home, Katya visited the doctor, who said there was only one baby.

Women were allowed — even encouraged — to have their babies, apart from the first one, at home as long as no problems were expected. The doctor told us that because we had followed his instructions, the child should be born on May 8th. The year was 1956. Katya fell twice while carrying this baby — once in the snow and a worse fall on the stairs. We were worried for the baby's sake but the nurse told us there was no way of knowing if it was okay. Katya also had her ears pierced when she was seven months pregnant — an act she regretted as soon as she had done it, in case it hurt the child. But the person who pierced her ears didn't use any anaesthetic, so we hoped all would be well.

When May 8th arrived, it seemed as if the doctor was wrong — the baby was not going to make an appearance. So I went to work as usual and my factory had asked me to do some overtime which I'd agreed to. The lady who lived over the back garden from us said she would keep an eye on Katya and Peter in case anything happened, but it looked as if it wasn't going to be the big day. We had a spare bedroom ready with Peter's old cot (near the bed Katya would be using) for the new baby. My wife was hoping for a girl, but I wanted another boy — we had decided that this would be our last child and I had always wanted sons. Another reason I wished for boys was to keep the Antonenko name going onwards.

In the late afternoon of May 8th, unbeknown to me, Katya went into labour. As we had no telephone she asked the lady who lived across the garden, Mrs Swanook, for help. Mrs Swanook tried to call my work but couldn't get through because I was working overtime and the girl who worked on the switchboard had gone home. So instead she called the midwife nurse, who was there in minutes. Our neighbour also took Peter to play with her children who were already his friends. When I arrived home I saw the nurse's car and realised that the baby must be on its way. As soon as I got in and washed my hands, the nurse asked me to help, which I was happy to do. She told me not to go in the bedroom where Katya was, but to get some hot water and towels. She kept me quite busy for a while. For a long time I stood outside the bedroom door, but I couldn't hear anything and wondered what was going on. I was getting anxious, then I heard the cry of a baby! I started to go into the room, but both Katya and the nurse told me the baby wasn't properly born yet and that as soon as it was, I could come and see it.

When I was eventually allowed in I was told that the child was a boy. The nurse had cleaned, weighed and dressed him and put him in the cot. I was told he weighed 8 3/4 lbs. When I saw him he was already asleep, but I could see he was a well-made baby with very white-blonde hair. I looked down on my new son asleep in his cot and I thought, 'Another boy, how beautiful he is.' I felt so happy I felt the tears come to my eyes. I said a silent prayer of thanks that both Katya and the baby were all right and my hopes that everything would continue to go smoothly. We thanked the nurse and I saw her out. She had left some instructions and told us she would visit again the next day, and for a while to come. I wanted to have a good look at the baby to see if he was okay, but Katya didn't want his sleep disturbed. (Later we found he had very light blue eyes and small dent in his ears in the same places where Katya had her ears pierced.)

As soon as I was sure Katya was okay, I went over to pick Peter up from Mrs Swanook's. I wanted him to see his new brother. When I thanked Mrs Swanook, she asked if she and her family could come to see Katya and the baby, but the nurse had told me that anyone else had to wait until the next day. When Peter first looked in the cot and saw the baby he said, 'Is it a boy or a girl?' When we said "boy" he didn't say anything — he knew he was going to have a baby brother or sister, but we never found out which he wanted.

We thought that no baby could be as noisy as Peter, but this baby had a very loud voice. Because he was so blonde he had trouble with his skin — even the smallest drop of urine made him sore. We did our very best to keep him as dry as possible and used powder and oil and anything else that we were told would help. We had a copper to boil the nappies to super clean, but it was difficult at times to get them dry. By this time Peter was two years and one month old and pretty well toilet trained, so nearly all the nappies were from the baby.

*　*　*

Katya insists that I mention that I helped her a lot with the children, even though I was working. I just did the best I could. I clipped the baby's finger and toenails as Katya was nervous of doing this because the nails were so small. I also washed many very dirty nappies by hand. We did have a copper to boil them in but they had to be washed first. I often saw Katya's fingers bleeding from doing washing by hand so I helped as much as I could. I also did household chores. I know Katya appreciated this. 'At that time men, especially British men, on the whole did not help in this way,' she says.

We still had to get up in the night to make baby formula while the baby screamed the house down — as had happened with Peter — and sometimes it was quite cold for us. Katya reminded me that I had promised to let her choose this baby's name. She had agreed that she would choose an Ukranian saint's name. When she wanted to call the child Martin, I thought it was too old fashioned, but my friends Inas and Cecillia — who were very happy to hear we had another son — wrote to say that in their opinion Martin wasn't an old-fashioned name at all. My bosses at work had already told me I could only have time off for our first child, but when Martin arrived, knowing we had no relatives living close by and would get very little help, they gave me a few days off with pay.

*　*　*

A few days after the baby's arrival I received a letter from the father of Mike, the best man at our wedding. Before I could open the letter Katya exclaimed, 'Mike's dead!' When I opened the letter and started reading it I found she was right — she got a shock because she had just said it without thinking and was surprised that she was right. His father's letter was very sad; I could see it was smudged with tears. He said Mike had been riding his motorbike and had hit a cow. He had been taken to hospital with a hair-line fracture of the skull and it seems he would have recovered, but he discharged himself.

This foolish act must have caused his death. His father had asked me to come to the funeral. Katya and I both felt absolutely terrible that I had to write back to him to say I couldn't because I had to look after Katya and our second son. We knew how terrible this was for him, because Mike and his father were the last members of their family still alive and his father had hoped that once they came to Britain Mike would marry and have children. Now the old man had lost his whole family. I was very sorry to hear of Mike's death, but not surprised, because he would drink too much and then ride.

When we had been in our council house for a while, the father of the people who had lived in the castle stopped me one day on my way to work. He talked for a while saying he was a train driver and he mentioned his family had been allotted a house just after us. I thought he was going to say there were no hard feelings, but he asked me if we would be willing to change houses with him. I told him I was sorry; we had bought carpet, stair carpet and curtains and had settled in. I added that if he had asked earlier we would have done so, because living on a steep hill did pose some difficulties.

One Saturday, when Martin was about three months old, Katya said she would like to see a certain film. She hadn't had time to go out for quite a while except shopping in the village. I suggested she go and I would look after the boys. While she was gone a man came to the door. When I answered it he said, 'I'm from the RSPCC and my organisation has received a complaint about you.'

I was surprised and answered, 'You must have come to the wrong house. We don't have any animals.' He then explained that his society cared for children and that they had received a complaint that we were not caring for our children properly. I was astounded; we lived for those kids and although we were reclusive and didn't really mix with the villagers, I felt that everyone knew this.

The man was apologetic, but said that when they received a complaint they had to check. He looked at everything; the nappies, the cot, Peter's bed, the sheets, blankets and everything to do with the children. He could see how fussy we were and couldn't find anything wrong. He told me so and asked where my wife was. I told him and he said, 'Someone will come and speak to your wife in a few days.' When she came home from the movies I tried to tell her as gently as possible what had happened. She couldn't believe it and really lost her temper. 'What if they take the children away from us?' she cried, and was worried the man might think she should have been there taking care of the children. She said, 'He would come on the one day I go out.' I had never seen her so upset. She asked who had done this to us but I didn't know. When I asked the man, he said he wasn't allowed to say. I thought, *it's a good thing we don't know at this time because Katya is so furious.* I suggested she go over and talk to Mrs Swanook (I think her first name was Grace) and Katya told me later that after her friend had tried to comfort her, she said that as she heard all the village gossip, she would find out who had done this to us.

Katya had been to a morning film so there was still plenty of the day left and it was still light. She said, 'I'm going for a walk.' This worried me because she seemed devastated; I knew she lived for those kids (and for me too, I hoped). I said, 'If you insist on going for a walk, take Peter with you.' I was sure she wouldn't do anything foolish if Peter was with her. I stayed behind to look after the baby who wasn't ready to go out.

When someone came to see Katya from the RSPCC it was a lady who was very nice. She found the children and their belongings spotless and couldn't find anything wrong. She told Katya that someone had told them the baby had a very loud cry and that they could hear him across the gardens when we put him outside in his pram. She could see he had a slightly sore bottom, but she agreed with Katya that the complaint was made out of spite. Doctor Green, who Katya had told what had happened, also told the organisation that we were fussy about the children and in his opinion it was a cruel hoax. He also told them that the village people knew how well we cared for the children and I believe that they did know, too.

We thought it may have been done because I was a foreigner and this turned out to be partly true. Mrs Swanook told Katya, and she also heard it from other sources, that it was the people who wanted our house who had reported us. They boasted about it and were reported to have said, 'Why should a foreigner have a council house?' Although they won in one way — this was the worst thing they could have done to us — they also lost, as most of the people in the village seemed to agree that it was a terrible thing to do. We were fairly sure it was these people — it was a very nasty thing to do, but we could see they thought they had a grievance, even though we had never intended to do them any harm. We had been fairly happy at the house but now we felt uneasy — we hated to think that people would do such a thing to us for spite.

* * *

Inas wrote to say he and Cecillia were applying to immigrate to Canada, where her mother was living. Because of the trouble with the people who reported us and my problems travelling to work and having no chance of another job, we thought we would try to immigrate to Canada too. We thought the climate might be better and that the children would have a better chance in life. In Britain in those days, if you were poor you couldn't better your lot even if you were British born, unless you were very clever or lucky. It was a big disadvantage being born in another country. I had decided to become a British citizen — not only in case we were picked for Canada but because I felt if I was going to live in a Western country it would be better for myself and my family if I became naturalised. So I applied, and in time was allowed to become a British citizen.

After a while we applied to immigrate to Canada. We didn't hear from them for ages and when they did reply we were rejected. Inas and Cecillia were accepted because they had relatives there. Also, Inas was a well-educated man — he was a writer and journalist and could also repair watches and clocks. This was his hobby but he was good enough to have done it professionally.

A few months after the incident with the RSPCC one of Katya's sisters, Billie, was having some personal problems and asked if she could stay with us for about a month. We agreed — we had enough room and I thought I got on with her family all right. Unfortunately, once she arrived I realised we just couldn't get on. We really seemed to annoy each other but for Katya's sake, I didn't ask her to leave. I thought she wouldn't be there very long and I was at work most of the time.

When Martin was six months old we decided it was time to have him christened. Inas and Cecilla were preparing to go to Canada and couldn't come but Billie was pleased to be his Godmother. But Inas wouldn't be Godfather, Mike was dead and I had lost touch with Nick, my groomsman, and I wanted a Ukranian to be Godfather. There was a man who still lived in Nescliff camp and, although he was much older than me, he was quite a good friend.

His name was Basil Matunenko and he had attended our wedding at the church and reception. He was very pleased to be asked to be Godfather but was worried he couldn't afford to buy the baby a golden cross, which it is usual for the Godfather to do. Inas had bought one for Peter. We didn't care about this, so I told him so and said I'd buy it. We were surprised and pleased, therefore, when he brought us a gift of a beautiful carpet-like wall hanging. Archbishop Molchanivski came to the house to perform the ceremony and we had a small party to celebrate. At Vidma's we'd had just a small meal for the priest and Godparents — we hadn't invited Vidma.

* * *

When Peter was six months old we visited a studio to have professional photos taken. They came out really well and the one we liked the photographer also liked — he said he would colour ours for no charge if we allowed him to use the photo for advertising in his main window. We were happy to show off the photo so the colouring — which was done by hand in those days and quite expensive — was an added bonus. When Martin was six months old we decided to have his photo taken by the same man. However when we made inquiries we found he had moved to another town, so we had to go to someone else. We couldn't afford to get Martin's photo coloured and Katya didn't like any of the photos. I thought one was quite good so we bought it, but Katya has never been really happy with it and really wanted colour.

Some health care person had suggested that Peter's feet were very flat and that he needed to go to the hospital for exercises. Once a week Katya had to walk there with the two children — it took all day. While Billie was with us she helped Katya manage, but when she left Katya had to do everything herself, including being out all day. She did this for a while, but most of the walking with the two children in the pram was on poor country footpaths. After a few months she told them that she couldn't manage to come in to the hospital now that her sister had left, so they gave her a list of exercises for Peter to do at home. Katya didn't mention it to the hospital staff, but she told me that although Peter was only two and a half he was upset about and sorry for the disabled children who were there for treatment. I believed this as I realised she understood him and I also knew he was sensitive.

We were still thinking of immigrating and our thoughts turned to America when Canada rejected us. We had just missed out on Canada — three months previously a law had been passed stating that a family wishing to immigrate had to have either a family member or another person willing to sponsor them living in the country. Alternately, there must be a job waiting for them — the job being one that the Canadian government needed workers for at that time. We made inquiries how to go about immigrating to America and were given some forms at the Labour Exchange, which we filled out and sent away to one of the American consulates. I believe it may have been in Liverpool. After this they wrote and asked us to send photos of the four of us and supply references from the chief of police in our district and from two doctors who knew us. We had no more correspondence after we had done that so we just waited — in fact we are still waiting — and we never heard any more on the matter. We knew if we were not accepted as migrants, we would never get to America because it was much too expensive. After a while Katya suggested we try Australia, but I had never considered Australia — I knew very little about it except that it was very hot, which I told her on more than one occasion. I gave it very little thought, believing we would eventually hear from the Americans.

While we were waiting for a reply from the Americans, I heard that a factory about forty-five miles away was looking for workers.

I can't remember the name of the town where the factory was but I was told that the pay was very good and, because the firm had about ten workers who lived in my area, they had their own bus. I thought this sounded just the thing for me — I needed more money with two children growing up and my transport problem would be solved. I took a day off from work and travelled to this factory to ask for a job. It was a type of forge where they made spare parts for machinery, cars and trucks. They needed more workers and hired me, so I gave my notice in at the plastic factory.

When I started work at the new place, I realised that about 2000 people worked there. My job was to bring materials on a hand-pushed trolley to the workers on the machines. The job wasn't bad but I got a big shock when I realised what the place was like. It was very big and very old, dark, dirty and very hot — full of fumes from the hot metal. The ventilation was very poor and the whole place smelt of burning oil and rubber. Oil had been spilt on the floors so often and never cleaned up that it felt soft — like rubber — when walked on. I don't know if there was a canteen, but the workers ate their food while sitting at their machines, not even washing their hands. It seemed as if conditions hadn't changed for hundreds of years. I found the place absolutely terrible, although I had no trouble with any of the people there. I stuck it out for two weeks, then I went back to the plastic factory and asked the big boss for my job back. He was very reluctant to give a job to someone who had left and gone somewhere else. I explained that I'd liked working there and had only left because of the difficulties of travelling to and from work. I found I was pleading saying, 'I have two small children to provide for.' I was almost crying. In the end he gave me my old job back. I really hated to beg like that but I'd always done what was really needed. I decided to forgive myself, thinking Katya and the boys were more important than pride.

After that our lives went on in the same way. The boys started to grow up into fine children. We were very happy with both of them. Martin walked and talked earlier in his life than Peter — maybe because Peter helped him with these things. They fought sometimes but were good healthy young boys. I spent as much time with the family as I could spare, but not as much as I would have liked — with money being short, I had to work as much as possible. Thankfully, Katya and the boys got on really well together. She was hardly ever away from them. As well as taking them out in the pram and the pusher, she would pull them on a sledge I made when the weather was very snowy under foot. The boys caught the usual childhood illnesses but we didn't have any real health crises. We travelled twice more to visit Katya's family, mostly so they could see the boys growing up. Their grandparents thought the boys were wonderful. We travelled both times by train. The second time Peter became ill on the train, but he soon recovered and when we arrived at Katya's parents' place we didn't even have to send for the doctor — we never knew what was wrong. He seemed so ill on the train.

When we got back home we still had the same problems. I had the difficulties of getting to and from work. Don't think I'm one to complain — I put up with a lot of things but this was a very difficult task, especially as we often had very bad weather. I also didn't earn enough money, resulting in us always owing the village shops money. Katya never let us get very far into debt. Although we adults didn't eat meat very often because it was so expensive, we always made sure the boys never went without anything and always had a variety of foods. Because I feel insecure if I don't have some money saved and because I still hoped we might emigrate, Katya tried to save a small amount each week. It was a few years since the incident with the RSPCC but we still felt uneasy, living in the same area as those people, even though they didn't do us further harm.

The happiest day of my life:
our wedding in Nescliffe, England, 1953

Andrii and best friend
Wasyl Dydai,
1950

*Andrii and Katya at an army
dance, Nescliffe,
England, 1952*

*Andrii and Inas Omelianenko,
1951*

BOOK IV

The Lucky Country

EPILOGUE

Andrii and Katya sought to immigrate to ensure a better life for their children, Peter and Martin. Andrii was attracted to the idea of moving to Canada because he perceived it to be like the Ukraine (and there were many Ukrainians already there) however their application to Canada, and later America, was unsuccessful. This was disheartening but they shortly after became aware of an 'assisted passage' scheme if they were prepared to immigrate to Australia.

They knew very little about Australia, other than an impression that it was supposed to be very hot. After doing some research they determined that some parts of Australia were not as hot as they believed and that one of these places, Melbourne, in the State of Victoria had plentiful work available. Despite not having any detailed appreciation of Melbourne or the likely difficulties involved, Andrii and Katya became more determined to pursue this option as they strongly felt staying in England was not the best thing for Peter and Martin.

After a successful interview at Australia House along with medicals attesting to the family's good health they were accepted and within weeks were on their way. There was a detail however that caused Andrii great concern, they were to be transported on a Russian ship. Even though it was very unlikely that the Russians would have even known who Andrii was, he was too suspicious to risk the journey. Katya was able to make an excuse without admitting Andrii's real concern, and the family was able to take an Italian ship later.

The hardships of those 'assisted passage' immigrants are difficult to relate to a modern audience. On the journey, the men and women were separated, accommodation was shared, the children staying with their mother. Conditions were cramped and the food very poor. Both the boys became very ill, and there was no medical attention. Katya spent all her time nursing them. On approaching their destination, the ship's authorities had advised them to pack everything other than light summer clothes because it would be a pleasant warm day. Contrary to this advice, they disembarked on the 8th of October 1959 to a wet and freezing Melbourne. The city had turned on a blustery rainy cold day to welcome them to their new life.

The family was lodged in two small rooms in a Nissen hut in an immigrant hostel in Brooklyn that was little better than the ship. Nissen huts being iron sheds, they were unbearably hot in the summer. The food was again dreadful, the accommodation was crowded and the shared washrooms dirty. Refuse tossed into open drains and food scraps left around the common areas attracted rats. The walls between themselves and the other tenants were paper thin, depriving anyone of privacy. Compounding all this unpleasantry the camp was beside a large abattoir, and frequently there was a foul stench hanging over the camp, particularly when the north wind blew.

Andrii was able to get a labouring job straight away with Rheem, an electric hot water systems manufacturer, less than ten minutes' walk away. Katya was also able to find work at Rheem. The wages in Australia were relatively very good to what they had experienced before, and they were able to quickly build up some money, enough to buy a small car. Given the poor state of public transport, a car was vital if they wanted to see anything beyond the immediate area of the camp.

Unsurprisingly, Andrii and Katya wanted to get out of the camp as soon as possible but they found landlords were unwilling to have them as tenants. They were compelled to live in the camp for two years. Eventually, they determined that if they wanted to get out of the hostel they would be compelled to buy a house. This too, proved to be a heartbreaking exercise. The only houses they could afford were in shabby areas and in poor condition. They did eventually find a house that was sound but superficially a mess. Andrii thought that he could do any repairs or renovations that were necessary.

While they did buy the house, it did come at a steep cost, the solicitor that organized the sale coerced them into signing an unconscionable mortgage. As if all the hardships of surviving communism and the War were not enough, being taken advantage of was a pattern that was to repeat itself throughout Andrii and Katya's early years in Australia. They were a quiet, shy people in a very unfamiliar place and their vulnerability was constantly abused by used car salesmen, dodgy loan companies, building merchants, dishonest tradesmen and mean tenants.

It was a tough life made tougher, but despite this despicable treatment, the family got by and made a life. They were resilient. They worked hard. They saved hard. They rented out rooms to help pay for their onerous mortgage, they bought second-hand toys for the boys, went on modest day trips to the beach for entertainment and were generally very frugal. They paid their debts, however unfair. They were committed and determined to give their sons the best life they could.

The boys grew into successful men. At an early age Peter became interested in being a pilot. He joined the air cadets as a boy, went on to graduate as a flight Captain in 1973 working from then on as a flying instructor and a commercial pilot, both in Australia and overseas. Martin went on to join the Airforce in 1974 and worked there for twenty years. Both married and had children, these grandchildren were the delight of Andrii and Katya's life.

A chance, and very emotional, meeting with a man who had lived in Andrii's village led to Andrii receiving a letter as to what had happened to his family. The letter told how after the war ended, his parents had been thrown out of the house again as soon as the communists were back in power. His parents roamed around from place to place, living with family and friends for periods of time, eventually being compelled to move on. This continued until Andrii's mother became blind from cataracts and couldn't keep on moving. Andrii's parents died shortly after this, years before Andrii received the letter. The letter went on to describe how the communists sentenced his youngest sister, Frossia, to ten years hard labour in a concentration camp. When she completed this sentence, she changed her name to a Russian one and moved away from the district. This letter also gave Andrii a vital connection that allowed him to write to and stay in touch with his sister and other relatives.

Andrii did often think about returning to the Ukraine after the fall of the Soviet Empire, but felt he couldn't, that from what he had read the people who had been communists were still in power and that his homeland had been destroyed by pollution made by the greed of the Russians and their collaborators.

After such a tumultuous life, Andrii and Katya enjoyed a quiet existence together after their boys left home. They went on simple, but to them grand holidays to Tasmania and to the Brisbane Expo. They spent time in the company of good friends, had much loved pets, adored their children, their children's partners and their grandchildren.

All aboard for Australia embarking on the Fairsea.

Our boys
Peter and Martin 1958

Our firstborn
Peter 1956

Crossing the line ceremony on the Fairsea

Katya, Peter and Andrii celebrate
Ukrainian Easter, 1980

Martin and Peter,
Air Force cadets, 1970

*Andrii, Peter and Martin,
1974*

Andrii, Peter, Katya, Samantha and Martin, 1982

*Peter flying for Fiji Air,
1984*

*Peter the Flying Instructor
at Laverton with Martin*

*Martin, Peter and
Andrii at Peter's
wings graduation
ceremony, 1973*

*Peter and Andrii in
the restored red MG
TD, 1994*

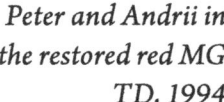

*Katya and Andrii,
Airlie Beach,
Queensland ... 1996*

*At Mary and
Harry's place,
1996*

*Andrii s 70th birthday,
1993, at Cuckoo
Restaurant in the
Dandenong Ranges*

Emily and her Grandad, 1994

The next generation Emily, Brian and Belinda at Peter and Amanda's house, 1997

Andrii and Brian at 14 months,
1987

Katya with Emily and William